This quarter, get excited as you and your kids follow Moses and the Israelites from Egypt to the Promised Land—from slavery to freedom! The Israelites came face to face with God's laws and salvation. They experienced God's wonderful grace, and so will you!

If this is your first time to teach this material or if you'd like a quick refresher, go to our website at gospellightsundayschool.com. But if you're ready to journey with the Israelites, then follow these easy 1-2-3 STEPS

Prepare and Pray

1. Check out the lesson introduction. The Big Idea tells why the lesson will make a difference in kids' lives—and in your life, too! The Action Plan helps you focus on what kids can do in this lesson to apply the Big Idea to life! Connecting You to Jesus shows how the action in this lesson's Bible story points to Jesus.

2. Read the lesson and customize it for your kids by marking the activities you plan to do. Pray for God to help you reach your kids and show His love to them.

3. Gather the materials you need—they're listed right there for you!

Teach

1. **Get Thinking:** Welcome your kids and use this activity to help them think about today's Big Idea!

2. **Get God's Word:** This is the heart and soul of your time together! Use the Story Starter to draw kids in and the fun Storytelling Idea to get kids participating as you tell the story.

3. **Get Talking:** Help kids talk about ways they can apply the Bible to their lives. Whiteboard Time, *Kid Talk Cards*, cool art activities and energetic games will keep your kids interacting with each other, with you and with God! (And get families talking, too, by handing out *Family Fridge Fun* papers for kids to take home.) End with a prayer time together!

Ready to journey to God's freedom? LET'S GO

CONNECT TO FAMILIES

Check out the Fall Family Event on the CD-ROM! This is a must-have event so that you can pump up parent participation in your program and help them grow faith at home. Get your parents started off right!

Contents

Articles

Lessons

 Gospel Light Sunday School Curriculum

Senior Managing Editor, Sheryl Haystead • **Senior Editor,** Deborah Barber • **Editor,** Rebecca English • **Video Clips,** Digital Felt Productions • **Editorial Team,** Mary Gross Davis, Kristina Fucci, Janis Halverson • **Contributing Writer,** Kurt Goble • **Designer,** Matthew Lawler

Founder, Dr. Henrietta Mears • **Publisher,** William T. Greig • **Senior Consulting Publisher,** Dr. Elmer L. Towns • **Editorial Director, Biblical and Theological Content,** Dr. Gary S. Greig

Find us on **Facebook**

CD-ROM

On the CD-ROM, you will find instructions for the Fall Family Event, teacher-training articles, Song Motion Charts and Lesson Extras such as game cards, patterns and more! Refer to "What to Print" on the CD-ROM.

Basic Supplies to Keep on Hand

Markers, pencils, paper (copy paper, construction paper, butcher paper, card stock, etc.), scissors, glue sticks, tape (clear and masking).

Materials Needed for Each Lesson

Bibles, whiteboard and markers, *Bible Teaching Poster Pack*, *Kid Talk Cards Grades 1 & 2*, *Family Fridge Fun* papers, *Get Going! Worship CD* and player, several copies of *What the Bible Is All About Bible Handbook for Kids;* optional—*Creative Clips DVD* and player.

Connecting Kids to Jesus

God's big picture of redemption throughout the Bible is the prime feature of this course! A focus on Jesus is in every lesson. Connecting You to Jesus, in the introduction of every lesson, will familiarize you with how the characters and the action of the lesson's Bible story point to Jesus and God's plan for salvation. These same concepts, written in kid-friendly words, are also part of each lesson's Wrap-Up: Connecting Kids to Jesus will give you the words to say to help your students see God's big plan for the ages—and how they can each be a part of that amazing plan!

But the best part of connecting kids to Jesus is helping them join His family! It's a huge joy—and it's easy! Here's a quick breakdown:

Pray. Start by praying for each kid you teach—keep a list on your phone or computer, in your prayer journal or in your Bible. Invite God to prepare each child to understand and receive His good news.

Talk one-on-one. Because kids are easily influenced to follow the group, be wise in the way you invite kids to join God's family when you're in a group setting. Make it easy for kids who express interest to talk and pray with a prepared adult—but without pressure.

Be clear. Kids need to understand the gospel! So we need to use words and phrases kids understand. And don't assume that they do understand just because they can repeat something back to you. Avoid symbolic terms ("born again," "ask Jesus to come into your heart," "open your heart," etc.). Those can confuse these literal-minded thinkers. (For some great words, check out the evangelism booklet *God Loves You!* It's available from Gospel Light.) Mark the Scriptures below. Read them aloud with an interested kid so that it's clear that joining God's family through repentance and faith in Jesus is God's big, beautiful idea!

Take Scripture Steps into God's Family

1. **God wants you to become His child. Why do you think God wants you in His family?** (See 1 John 3:1.)
2. **You and I and every person in the world have done wrong things. The Bible word for doing wrong is "sin." What do you think should happen to us when we sin?** (See Romans 6:23.)
3. **God loves you so much that He sent His Son to die on the cross to take the punishment for your sin. Because Jesus never sinned, He is the only One who can take the punishment for your sin. On the third day after Jesus died, what happened?** (See 1 Corinthians 15:3-4; 1 John 4:14.)
4. **Are you sorry for your sin? Tell God that you are. Do you believe Jesus died for your sin and then rose again? Tell Him that, too. If you tell God you are sorry for your sin and believe that Jesus died to take your sin away, what does the Bible say God will do?** (See 1 John 1:9.)
5. **The Bible says that when you believe that Jesus is God's Son and that He is alive today, you receive God's gift of eternal life. This gift makes you a child of God. This means God is with you now and forever!** (See John 1:12; 3:16.)

Another approach is to give each child in your class a copy of *God Loves You!* and read through the booklet together as a group. Ask, "What did you thnk about the booklet? What do you think is the most important part of the booklet? After reading the booklet, how would you describe Jesus?"

Celebrate! Encourage! Disciple!

YES! You have permission to be excited when a kid joins God's family! Encourage those kids to tell their family. Give their names to your pastor. And don't leave any babies to fend for themselves! Make yourself available to help them grow, or find another adult who will help them. Use the discipling booklet *Following Jesus* (available from Gospel Light) as a simple, effective way to help kids think about ways to grow in God's family.

TIP

Telling the good news about Jesus includes demonstrating Jesus' love. Every child should feel secure and loved in the church family. For the child whose home situation has not fostered feelings of love, you need to make special efforts to give extra attention. Be sure to notice and encourage the child's actions. Use the child's name frequently as you chat. Be interested in what he or she has to say. Listen attentively. These actions all build loving relationships. And loving relationships are what God's family is all about! Show the love of Jesus in a way that a child can see and understand.

Rescue on the Nile

Dear Teacher,

I was in the grocery store, doing routine errands, but I wasn't having a routine day. I was fearful and worried about something going on in my life and it showed on my face! As I went through the checkout, the cashier looked at me and said, with some irritation, "It's not that bad!" Her comment didn't make me feel better—but it got me thinking. I realized that when I let fear get the better of me, I can't be much of a blessing to others. I am too focused on myself!

One of my favorite verses is 1 John 4:18. It says that "perfect love drives out fear." That is so comforting to me! It means I can take the fears that make me turn inward and entrust them to a God who loves me and cares about my life. Then His love will fill me and give me rest. Instead of being anxious, I can be a channel of Christ's love to others!

Becky English
Editor

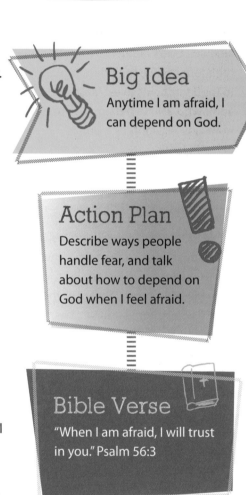

Big Idea
Anytime I am afraid, I can depend on God.

Action Plan
Describe ways people handle fear, and talk about how to depend on God when I feel afraid.

Bible Verse
"When I am afraid, I will trust in you." Psalm 56:3

Get God's Word (15-25 minutes)

Rescue on the Nile

Tell the following story summary in your own words, asking discussion questions as indicated.

Story Starter

If you had something really important to hide, where would you put it? Give several kids a chance to answer. Then repeat each answer, pausing after each and inviting all students to vote for their favorite answer by clapping for the one they choose. **You have some good ideas! In our story today, a woman had something VERY important to hide—her baby boy! And she hid her baby in the Nile River! Our story today is from the second book of the Bible, the book of Exodus.** Help students find Exodus 2 in their Bibles. **Let's listen to find out why the Nile River was the perfect hiding spot.**

> **YOU NEED**
>
> Bible for yourself and each student, Lesson 1 Poster, long and round balloons, permanent markers, flashlight.

STORYTELLING IDEA

Ahead of time, blow up five balloons. Draw a face on each balloon to represent Pharaoh, mother, baby, little girl, princess (see photo on next page). Use balloons to act out Bible story as directed.

Joseph's Family

Joseph, who God had made an important leader in Egypt, brought his father Jacob and the rest of his family to live with him in Egypt. The years went by, and babies and grandbabies were born. Joseph and his brothers died, but the family kept growing. Pretty soon, 70 people had become a whole nation—the nation of Israel!

> **TIP**
>
> Read aloud information about the title of the book of Exodus on page 35 in *What the Bible Is All About for Kids*.

Oppressed Family

After so many years, the Egyptians had forgotten about the good things Joseph had done for them. When a new king (called Pharaoh) began to rule Egypt, he didn't know about Joseph at all. He just knew there were a LOT of Israelites! And that made him worry. *What if this huge group of people joins our enemies in a war?* Pharaoh may have thought. *What if they fight us and then LEAVE?* So Pharaoh came up with a very bad plan. **Listen as I read Exodus 1:9-11 to hear what Pharaoh had his people do to the Israelites.** Show Pharaoh balloon.

The Egyptians made the Israelites work VERY hard for them. They treated the Israelites badly. But no matter how mean the Egyptians were, more and more Israelite babies were being born! The Israelite nation just kept GROWING! This made the Egyptians MORE scared.

So Pharaoh decided to do something terrible. He decided to KILL some of the Israelites! He told the midwives—women who helped when Israelite babies were born—that any time a BOY baby was born, they had to KILL him! **What do you think the midwives were going to do?**

Well, the midwives weren't going to kill babies. They must have felt afraid to disobey Pharaoh, but they trusted God and they let the boy babies live. God was kind to the midwives for saving the babies. He gave them families of their own!

Pharaoh realized that his plans were not working. So he came up with his worst idea yet. Since the midwives wouldn't kill the baby boys, Pharaoh gave an order to the people. He told them, "Every boy that is born you must throw into the Nile." Pharaoh really wanted to get rid of Israelite baby boys!

Courageous Family

Now about this time, one Israelite family had a baby boy. The baby's parents were scared

Big Idea

Anytime I am afraid, I can depend on God.

that the king might find the baby. But his mother was NOT going to throw her newborn son into the Nile River! Show mother balloon and baby balloon. She saw how fine a baby he was, and she hid him.

But after three months, she couldn't hide the baby any longer. **What do you think she did then?** She made a basket from plants called reeds and painted it with tar to make it waterproof. She put the baby inside, took the basket to the Nile and set it near the edge of the water. Rock baby balloon. She didn't want to leave her baby, but she had to trust God to take care of him. She told Miriam, the baby's big sister, to hide in the reeds and watch to see what would happen! Show little girl balloon hiding and watching baby balloon.

> **TIP**
>
> Show Lesson 1 Poster and ask a volunteer to tell what the princess might have been thinking in the picture.

Royal Family

Well, before long, something DID happen! Pharaoh's daughter came to the river to take a bath—and she saw the basket! Show princess and baby balloons. When the princess opened the basket, she saw the cute, crying baby! She felt sorry for him. **What do you think Miriam did?** Miriam stepped bravely out of the reeds and went up to the princess. Show little girl balloon talking to princess balloon. "Shall I get a woman to take care of the baby for you?" she asked.

Pharaoh's daughter thought this was a good idea. So Miriam went to their own MOTHER and brought her to the princess. The princess told the mother to take care of the baby. Show mother, princess and little girl balloons together. The princess even offered to PAY her to take care of the baby—her own little boy!

When the baby grew older, his mother took him to Pharaoh's palace and gave him to the princess! Show mother giving baby to princess. Pharaoh's daughter adopted the little boy as her own son, and she named him Moses. God would use Moses' adopted family to prepare him for a big job that he would do someday!

Pharaoh was afraid of the Israelites, so he was cruel to them. The midwives and Moses' mother and Miriam were probably afraid, too, because Pharaoh was being so mean, but they did not respond to their fear in bad ways like Pharaoh did. Instead, they chose to depend on God and do what was right.

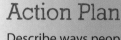

Action Plan

Describe ways people handle fear, and talk about how to depend on God when I feel afraid.

All of us feel afraid sometimes! But we don't have to respond to fear in wrong ways. Show the flashlight. If you've ever been in a dark, scary place and couldn't see, you know how good it is to have a flashlight to depend on! When we feel afraid and can't see what's going to happen, we can trust in something much better than a flashlight! Read aloud Psalm 56:3. We can depend on God and keep doing what is right! He loves to help us when we trust in Him.

Connecting Kids to Jesus

Moses was born to save God's people, the Israelites, from the pharaoh in Egypt. Moses reminds us of Jesus. Jesus was born to save ALL people from their sin.

Get Talking

(25-30 minutes)

Whiteboard Time 🖊

On whiteboard, write the word "afraid" and read it aloud. **What does this word mean?** Invite volunteers to tell words that mean the same as "afraid" ("worried," "scared," "upset," etc.). Write responses on whiteboard. Then write the word "trust," and invite volunteers to tell words that mean the same as this word ("hope," "believe," "depend on," etc.). **The words "afraid" and "trust" are in Psalm 56:3, our Bible verse.**

Distribute Lesson 1 *Kid Talk Cards* and ask students to look at Side 1. Read Bible verse aloud. **When we feel afraid, God wants us to trust in Him. When we depend on God, we can go from feeling scared to feeling hopeful. We know that He will take care of us.** Invite students to circle the names of the people in the story who they think trusted in God.

> **In today's story, how did some people do what Psalm 56:3 says to do?** (Moses' mother trusted God to take care of her baby as he floated on the river. Miriam was brave when she talked to the princess.)

> **Why do you think Pharaoh did NOT trust God?** (He was afraid of the Israelites. He wanted to control the Israelites.)

> **What are ways people act when they are afraid?** (Run away. Get angry. Call for help. Sing a song. Pray.)

Students look at Side 2 of *Kid Talk Cards*. Students cross out the *X*s and *Z*s to find out ways they can depend on God.

> **What are some ways we can depend on God?** (Pray. Read the Bible. Keep doing what is right, even if we feel afraid.)

> Point to photo of flashlight. **If you're in a dark place, it's important to have a flashlight to depend on! Sometimes we feel scared, like when we're in the dark. But we can depend on God. We can trust Him to help us!**

> **Why does God want us to depend on Him?** (He loves us! He is powerful and good. He does what is best. He can give us the help we need.)

Prayer

Invite volunteers to tell prayer requests as you write them on the whiteboard. Then pray with students about the needs and concerns they mention. Invite each student to tell times a kid might be afraid. As you briefly pray again, mention students' ideas.

Art

Give each student two sheets of craft foam in the colors of their choice. Students take turns using card-stock patterns to trace finger shape onto both sheets of craft foam and cut out. Each student spreads glue on one shape and lays paint-stirring stick on glue to make a handle. Student spreads more glue on stick and presses second shape onto first shape and onto stick. Students use markers to print "Trust in God!" or "God will help me!" or another slogan about trusting God on front of shape. Students use markers and other items as desired to decorate shape.

YOU NEED

Several copies of Foam Finger Pattern (from CD-ROM) printed on card stock and cut out, craft foam sheets in various colors, scissors, markers, paint-stirring sticks, glue sticks.

Connect: **God knows that we all feel afraid sometimes. That's why He tells us to trust in Him during scary times. I'm glad that God loves us! He is so kind and wants to help us when we're afraid.**

TIP

To make a giant foam finger, enlarge pattern 200 percent. Omit stick, and glue foam together around side and top edges only so that shape can be worn on hand.

Game

Ahead of time, use masking tape to make start and finish lines on the floor.

YOU NEED

Masking tape, two paper plates, two Ping-Pong balls.

Divide group into two teams. The first runner on each team places a Ping-Pong ball on a paper plate. Runners hold plates waiter-style (students can use two hands if necessary). First runners carry plates to the far line and then back to tag next teammates. Play continues until the whole team has completed the relay. (If a player drops the ball, he or she picks it up, puts it back on the plate and continues.) The first team to finish wins.

Connect: **When you were running, what did you worry about? Maybe you worried that your Ping-Pong ball might fall. Maybe you weren't REALLY worried. But in real life, we do worry and feel afraid at times. God doesn't want us to be afraid, though! He wants us to trust in Him and to remember that He will help us.**

Get Going

Direct students to look at Side 2 of their *Kid Talk Cards* again. **No matter how scary a situation is, God ALWAYS has a way for you to trust in Him! He will never leave you alone or forget to help you.** Play "I Will Trust in You" (track 4 on *Worship CD*), inviting students to listen or sing along. **This week, remember that God is with you. You can put all your trust in Him!** Distribute Lesson 1 *Family Fridge Fun* papers as students leave.

A Burning Bush

Dear Teacher,

In at least a small way, I think many of us can relate to Moses' fear of following God's call. God called Moses to step WAY out of his comfort-in-the-desert-with-the-sheep zone to challenge the world's most powerful leader and guide a giant group of opinionated people. Sounds scary!

A number of years ago, I had the opportunity to start a ministry for foster kids. I had no doubt that starting the ministry was what God wanted. But I doubted that I was the right person for the job. Surely there was someone else—someone more qualified, someone others would want to follow. But God continued to say that He wanted me for the job. So I finally obeyed. And God led in amazing ways, supplying every need and teaching me to trust Him like never before. Following God, even when we don't think we measure up, is an exciting way to live!

Debbie Barber

Senior Editor

Big Idea

God gives me confidence to follow Him, even when I think I'm not good enough.

Action Plan

List words that describe God, and discuss reasons to have confidence in Him.

Bible Verse

"Blessed is the man who trusts in the Lord, whose confidence is in him." Jeremiah 17:7

Connecting You to Jesus

God announced His name to Moses at the burning bush: "I Am Who I Am" (Exodus 3:14). The use of this name demonstrated God's character as unchanging, faithful and dependable. It showed that God wanted His people to trust in Him. And when Jesus later used the name, He was declaring Himself to be not just a wise teacher or a prophet but the same faithful and dependable "I Am" (John 8:58).

LESSON MATERIALS

- The basics (see contents)
- Life vest
- Get Thinking—cups and coffee mugs, Ping-Pong ball
- Story props (see p. 19)
- Materials for Art or Game activity (see pp. 24-25)

Lesson Extras!

1. Help your kids learn the order of the books in the Bible by playing Line Up the Books (on CD-ROM). Use only the first five books of the Old Testament for this lesson.

2. Students talk about today's Bible story as they complete Lesson 2 Bible Story Coloring Page (on CD-ROM).

3. DVD Option: **Sometimes people get confused about confidence. They think that acting confident is more important than who they have confidence in!** Show "Lesson 2: Confidence Guy" on *Creative Clips DVD*. **According to Jeremiah 17:7, where should Confidence Guy learn to find his confidence?**

Get Thinking

(10-15 minutes)

Welcome students and help them begin to think about today's Big Idea.

Ping-Pong Toss

Place several different cups and coffee mugs together on a table. Students take turns standing next to the table and attempting to toss a Ping-Pong ball into cups and/or mugs. After several attempts, challenge students to toss Ping-Pong ball in different ways (stand farther away, toss with eyes closed, bounce the ball once, etc.).

Big Idea

God gives me confidence to follow Him, even when I think I'm not good enough.

Connect:

> Tossing a Ping-Pong ball into a small cup can be challenging! What are some even harder things you have done?

> What are some things people do to prepare for hard or challenging tasks? (Practice. Try to get out of doing them. Ask for help.)

YOU NEED

Several different cups and coffee mugs, Ping-Pong ball.

> Today we're going to talk about how we can have confidence, even when we feel like we are not good enough!

Get God's Word (15-25 minutes)

A Burning Bush

Tell the following story summary in your own words, asking discussion questions as indicated.

Story Starter

Let's see if we can say a tongue twister together. First, listen to me as I say the tongue twister. Repeat the following tongue twister several times and then invite students to say it with you: **A big black bug bit a big black bear and made the big black bear bleed blood.** Then invite a few students to try repeating the tongue twister on their own. **Saying tongue twisters is fun. But when we are nervous, we can sometimes have a hard time saying what we want to say. In our story today, someone was afraid of getting tongue-tied when he talked.** Help students find Exodus 4:10 in their Bibles and find the words "I am slow of speech and tongue." **Listen to find out who said this, and why.**

> ### YOU NEED
> Bible for yourself and each student, Lesson 2 Poster, paper in different colors (brown, orange, green), life vest.

STORYTELLING IDEA

As you tell the story, tear colored paper into simple shapes as directed. Show shapes to students to illustrate the story.

Prince of Egypt

Moses was an Israelite, but he grew up in the Egyptian royal family. All the other Israelites were slaves of the Egyptians! As slaves, the Israelites had to work hard—and they were not treated well at all!

One day when Moses was about 40 years old, he went out to the area where the Israelites were living. He saw that some of the Egyptians were being mean to the Israelites. And as he stood there watching them work,

> ### TIP
> Read aloud information about Moses on page 36 in *What the Bible Is All About for Kids*.

he saw an Egyptian beating an Israelite—one of Moses' own people! Tear brown paper to make a frown shape.

Moses was so angry that he killed the Egyptian! Moses tried to keep what he had done a secret, but someone had seen—and the news about what Moses had done started to spread. And UH-OH—it had spread even to the palace!

What do you think Pharaoh wanted to do about Moses? Moses knew he was in BIG trouble if he stayed—so he ran! He kept running until he got to a place called Midian, over the border from Egypt. He hid out in the wild, empty places of Midian for 40 YEARS! During that time, Moses got a job taking care of sheep in the desert. Moses probably never expected to go back to Egypt again.

God's Call to Moses

But even while Moses was hiding out in Midian, God knew where he was. And God had a plan for Moses! During that time, the Israelites began to cry out to God and pray for His help. They asked God to get them out of slavery! Of course, God had not forgotten them. No, He had been working out His plan to free the Israelites from slavery! For 80 YEARS, God had been preparing someone to LEAD the Israelite slaves out of Egypt: Moses!

How do you think Moses found out about his new job? God had a brilliant and simple solution. As Moses led his sheep near Mount Horeb one day, he noticed that a bush was on fire. Tear orange paper to make a flame shape. But the bush wasn't burning down into ashes—it just kept burning! Moses came closer to see what was going on. Then GOD'S voice SPOKE to him from the bush! God called Moses by name!

Listen as I read Exodus 3:6-7 to find out what God told Moses! God had chosen MOSES to go to Egypt and demand that the new Pharaoh let the Israelites leave! **How do you think Moses felt about his new job?** Moses was afraid! God

Big Idea

God gives me confidence to follow Him, even when I think I'm not good enough.

reminded Moses that HE would be with him. God told Moses His own name: I Am Who I Am! That should have been enough for Moses—only the one true God could have THAT name! But Moses STILL had lots of questions!

God told Moses to go to the Israelite leaders first and get their help. God also gave Moses power to do miracles. God gave Moses power to make his stick into a snake by throwing it down. *Tear green paper to make a snake shape.* God gave Moses power to make his hand infected with leprosy and then make it healthy again! *Tear brown paper to make a hand shape.*

But Moses still wasn't convinced! He complained that he wasn't good at speaking. He whined until God had had ENOUGH! God told Moses that He would send Moses' brother Aaron to speak for Moses. Then Moses wouldn't have to talk, but he would still have to do the miracles.

> **TIP**
>
> Show Lesson 2 Poster and ask students to tell what they would have said at the burning bush.

Back to Egypt

It was time to return to Egypt. So Moses went home, packed up his family and started for Egypt. Aaron met him on the way so they could go to Egypt together. When they brought all the Israelite leaders together, they told them what God had said and showed them the miracles God had given Moses power to do. When the leaders heard how God cared about them in their misery, they bowed and worshiped God.

Wrap-Up

Moses eventually learned to have confidence in God instead of worrying about things he didn't think he could do. Moses felt like his big job of talking to Pharaoh and leading God's people was too much. He must have felt like he was in over his head! But God was right there, giving him everything he needed to follow God's instructions.

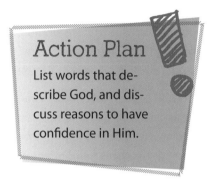

Action Plan

List words that describe God, and discuss reasons to have confidence in Him.

Show life vest. **When I wear a life vest like this, I feel more confident in the water. And when I remember God's promises, I have confidence to follow God, no matter what happens or how much I'm afraid that I'm not good enough. That confidence in God makes me glad!** Read Jeremiah 17:7 aloud. **You can have trust and confidence in God's help, too! As you do the things you know God wants you to do, God will help you and give you everything you need, just like He did for Moses!**

Connecting Kids to Jesus

When God talked to Moses at the burning bush, He showed Moses that He is unchanging, faithful and dependable. God said that His name was "I Am Who I Am." Later, in the New Testament, Jesus used the same name for Himself. Jesus was telling the people that He really is the one true God and that we can always trust in Him!

 **(25-30 minutes)**

Whiteboard Time

On whiteboard, print "yppah." Students read the word backwards ("happy"), and a volunteer writes it correctly on the whiteboard. Then print "no sdneped" on whiteboard. Students read words backwards to discover phrase "depends on." A volunteer writes the words correctly on the whiteboard. **These words tell us what two of the words in our Bible verse mean.** Read Jeremiah 17:7 aloud and invite students to guess which words in the verse mean the same as "happy" and "depends on." **Trusting in God's help is a great thing to do and helps us be happy!**

Distribute Lesson 2 *Kid Talk Cards* and ask students to look at Side 1. Read the Bible verse. **Choose a door and follow the path to a sentence starter to complete!**

▷ **Why do you think Moses had a hard time trusting in God and doing what God told him to do?**

▷ **What are some reasons kids today might have a hard time trusting in God?**

▷ **How did Moses show that he had learned to trust in God?** (Talked to Pharaoh, even though he was not good at talking. Led the people out of Egypt.)

Students turn to Side 2 of *Kid Talk Cards*. **Search the picture to find some great reasons to have confidence in God!**

▷ Point to photo of life vest. **Life vests help people feel more brave when they are in deep water, but God is so much better than a life vest! He loves us and has the power to help us in every situation!**

▷ **What words did you find? Which one is your favorite to describe God? Why do you like that description of God?**

▷ **Other than the words in our puzzle, what are reasons that people have confidence in God?** (They remember how God has helped them in the past. They have heard about great things He has done.)

Prayer

Invite students to take turns praying short prayers using a word that describes God and then thanking Him for that quality. Then invite volunteers to tell prayer requests as you write them on the whiteboard. Pray with students about the needs and concerns they mention.

Art

Ahead of time, print on large sheet of paper phrases that tell reasons to have confidence in God ("God is good," "God loves me," "God has power," etc.).

Give each student a craft-foam strip. Students choose a phrase from the large sheet of paper to copy onto craft-foam strip. Then students decorate strips as desired to make bracelets. Help students use a paper fastener to attach a craft-foam circle shape at one end of strip. Then cut a lengthwise slit in the other end of strip to make a buttonhole. Help students attach ends, using the craft-foam circle as a button. Encourage students to wear bracelets as reminders to have confidence in God.

Connect: **Each time you see your bracelet, you can remember to be brave and obey God in everything you do. God will always help you and care about you!**

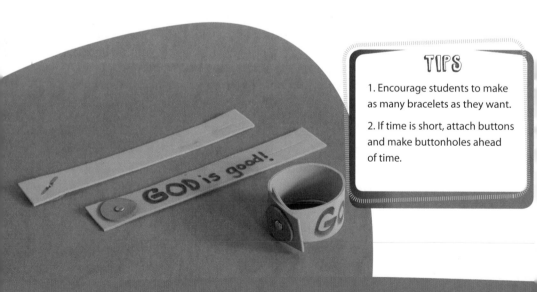

TIPS

1. Encourage students to make as many bracelets as they want.

2. If time is short, attach buttons and make buttonholes ahead of time.

Game

Students sit in a circle. Give ball to one student. Student tosses the ball to any other student in the group. As soon as student tosses the ball, he or she gets up and begins to run around the circle. Student who caught the

YOU NEED
Ball.

ball quickly passes the ball to student next to him or her, and students continue passing ball around the circle. Students attempt to get the ball back to the student who caught it before the runner returns to his or her seat. Student who wins (either the runner or the student who caught the ball) completes the sentence "I have confidence in God because . . ." Repeat game as time permits, giving ball to a different student to start each round.

Connect: **Because of who God is, we can trust God's love and care for us all the time! This week, I hope you'll remember to feel brave and be confident in following God, no matter what happens or how you feel.**

Get Going

Direct students to look at Side 2 of their *Kid Talk Cards* again. **I'm so glad that we can trust God and have confidence in Him, no matter how we feel about ourselves!** Play "I Will Trust in You" (track 4 on *Worship CD*), inviting students to listen or sing along. **Let's remember this week to pray for each other to be brave enough to follow God, even when we think we are not good enough.** Distribute Lesson 2 *Family Fridge Fun* papers as students leave.

Out of Egypt

Dear Teacher,

As I read through the plagues in Exodus, I'm struck by the idea that God is SERIOUS about dealing with our sin and our desire to follow other gods. In Exodus 5 through 12, God showed Himself to be greater than every god the Egyptians worshiped, turning each area of their idol worship and/or dependence into a repulsive thing.

What would my life be like if God chose to do that with each and every thing that I allow to get in the way of worshiping God? What a sobering thought! God has every right to force my love and worship—He is holy and fully worth so much more than I could ever give. But He patiently forgives each and every sin in my life—every time! Each time I turn away from following God and then turn back again, Jesus' forgiveness is there. He covers my sin with His blood, presenting me as righteous before God. Now that is truly amazing!

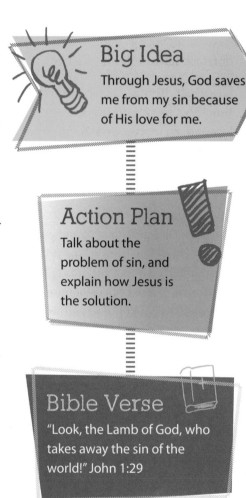

Big Idea

Through Jesus, God saves me from my sin because of His love for me.

Action Plan

Talk about the problem of sin, and explain how Jesus is the solution.

Bible Verse

"Look, the Lamb of God, who takes away the sin of the world!" John 1:29

Debbie Barber

Senior Editor

Connecting You to Jesus

Exodus 12 gives us the thrilling story of the Passover, the clearest Old Testament picture of our salvation through faith in the shed blood of our Lord Jesus Christ. The events of this chapter gave John the Baptist the basis for calling Christ "the Lamb of God." Christ is our Passover Lamb. Jesus gave His life so that all who believe in Him could be rescued from certain death and the slavery of sin. Faith in Jesus makes us truly free and part of God's family forever!

LESSON MATERIALS

- The basics (see contents)
- Cross
- Get Thinking—swim ring
- Story Starter—Coin Problem sheet (from CD-ROM), nine coins
- Materials for Art or Game activity (see pp. 34-35)

Lesson Extras!

1. Help your kids learn the order of the books in the Bible by playing Line Up the Books (on CD-ROM). Use only the first 12 books of the Old Testament for this lesson.

2. Students learn about today's Bible verse by completing Lesson 3 Bible Verse Puzzle (on CD-ROM).

3. DVD Option: **Let's see if you can figure out what these signs warn people about.** Show "Lesson 3: Warning Signs" on *Creative Clips DVD*. **When God's people were slaves in Egypt, God gave Pharaoh lots of warnings.**

Get Thinking  (10-15 minutes)

Welcome students and help them begin to think about today's Big Idea.

Ring Rolling

Make two parallel masking-tape lines on the floor. Students stand at either end of the lines and take turns rolling swim ring, attempting to make it roll between the lines to the other end. Any student at the far end rolls swim ring back.

Big Idea

Through Jesus, God saves me from my sin because of His love for me.

Connect:

⟩ **What are swim rings usually used for?**

⟩ **How might a swim ring be helpful when some-one gets tired in deep water?** (The person can hold onto the swim ring and stay above the water.)

⟩ **Swim rings can be used to help rescue people in the water. Today we'll be talking about how God has rescued us!**

YOU NEED

Masking tape, swim ring.

Get God's Word (15-25 minutes)

Out of Egypt

Tell the following story summary in your own words, asking discussion questions as indicated.

Story Starter

On table, arrange nine coins into a triangle as shown on Coin Problem sheet. Show coins to students. **Here's a problem for you to solve: Move just two coins to form a square.** Volunteers attempt to form a square by moving only two coins. After several attempts, demonstrate how to make a square, following the directions on the Coin Problem sheet. **This was a fun problem to solve! But our Bible story today tells about a real and important problem and how God solved it in an amazing way! It all started with a man whose name is in Exodus 5:1.** Help students find Exodus 5:1 in their Bibles and point to the name Moses. **Let's find out what happened!**

> **YOU NEED**
>
> Bible for yourself and each student, Lesson 3 Poster, Coin Problem sheet (from CD-ROM), nine coins, cross.

STORYTELLING IDEA

As you tell the story, guide students to pantomime story actions.

A Demand Made

The Israelites were slaves in Egypt. They had to work and work. Students pound fists onto palms of other hands several times. Moses and Aaron went to see Pharaoh. They said, "This is what the Lord, the God of Israel, says: 'Let my people go!'"

Well! Pharaoh didn't care about the God of the Israelites! He said, "Who is the Lord that I should obey

HIM? I don't know Him, and I WON'T let Israel go!" Then Pharaoh decided to make the slaves work even HARDER so that they weren't distracted by this talk about leaving. Students pound fists faster.

Soon the Israelites told Moses, "You've made a mess of things! Now Pharaoh and his men want to kill us with MORE work!" Students make grumpy faces.

Powerful Plagues

What do you think Moses did? Moses prayed! Students pretend to pray. God told Moses that all he needed to do was obey. When Moses returned to Pharaoh, he did miracles to show that God was the one true God. But Pharaoh's heart was hard. He would NOT let the Israelites go! So God began to send plagues on Egypt.

TIP

Show Lesson 3 Poster and ask students to tell what they think the people other than Pharaoh were thinking.

First, the water turned to blood! **What would you think if our water turned to blood?** Students make disgusted faces. But this didn't change Pharaoh's mind. Then God sent frogs—frogs in the beds, in the food, in the ovens—everywhere! This annoyed Pharaoh enough that he told Moses, "If you'll make the frogs go away, I'll let the people go." So except for the frogs in the Nile, all of the frogs DIED. And they STANK. But then Pharaoh changed his mind!

So God sent gnats everywhere. Students pretend to shoo away gnats. Then God sent big flies, LOTS of big flies. But the flies were ONLY in the homes and palaces of the Egyptians! The flies stayed away from the Israelites.

Pharaoh said he'd let the people go if God would remove the flies. Moses prayed. And God did what Moses asked. But Pharaoh changed his mind again! Moses warned Pharaoh that things were going to get worse, but Pharaoh didn't care.

Next all of the Egyptians' livestock got sick. But not even ONE of the Israelites' animals was ill! Then

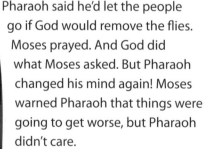

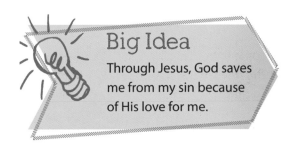

Big Idea

Through Jesus, God saves me from my sin because of His love for me.

both the Egyptian people and their animals got horrible sores on them. Students pretend to scratch. Then there was terrible hail. The Egyptians' crops were ruined! But the plants of the Israelites were undamaged! Locusts and darkness followed for the Egyptians. But the Israelites' homes and fields were protected. And Pharaoh? He still stayed stubborn!

We're Free!

Finally, God told Moses that He was sending a plague that would convince Pharaoh to let the Israelites go. God's people needed to be ready. When this plague hit, it would be time to move right away!

> ### TIP
> Read aloud information about the Passover Lamb on page 36 in *What the Bible Is All About for Kids*.

The Israelites did just as God told them: Each family took a perfect male lamb and marked their doorposts with its blood. They roasted and ate the lamb meat, wearing their coats, ready to go. Students stand and pretend to eat. This meal was called Passover because the lamb's blood on the door kept everyone in that house safe. But in any house where a door wasn't marked, all the firstborn died. People, birds, animals—all the firstborn died, even in Pharaoh's palace.

In the middle of the night, stubborn Pharaoh finally summoned Aaron and Moses. "Up!" he shouted. "Leave my people! Go!"

So the Israelites left, moving out into the darkness of the desert. **How do you think the Israelites felt?** They were following God to the land He had promised to Abraham, Isaac and Jacob. God was keeping His promise and leading His people to the Promised Land. Students walk in place, and then sit back down.

Wrap-Up

God rescued His people in an amazing way! He helped all the people know that He was really the one true God. God's rescue of the Israelites from the last plague is something that Jewish people have celebrated every year since that time! And this celebration, called Passover, was the very same holiday that Jewish people were celebrating when Jesus was killed on a cross many, many years after our story today took place.

Show cross and read John 1:29 aloud. **Jesus was called the Lamb of God because He is God's perfect Son, and His death on the cross made the way for God to forgive the sin of all the people who believe in Him.** Talk with interested students about salvation (see "Connecting Kids to Jesus" article on pp. 3-5).

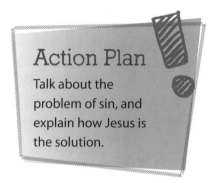

Action Plan

Talk about the problem of sin, and explain how Jesus is the solution.

Connecting Kids to Jesus

The Passover is more than something that happened to the Israelites many, many years ago. It is also a picture of how God made a way for us to be saved by Jesus, the Lamb of God. Without God's forgiveness, we can't escape from the penalty of our sin. It's as if we are in slavery, just like the Israelites were. But when Jesus died on the cross, He paid the price for all the wrong things we have done. When we trust in Jesus, we are truly free and part of God's family forever!

   **(25-30 minutes)**

Whiteboard Time

On whiteboard, print keywords or phrases from John 1:29 ("look," "lamb," "takes away the sin" and "world"). Students suggest symbols for each word or phrase (eyes, lamb, cross, globe, etc.). Draw symbols next to the appropriate words on the whiteboard. **The Bible has lots of names for Jesus, but John 1:29 tells us one of His names: Lamb of God. Why do you think John called Him that?**

Distribute Lesson 3 *Kid Talk Cards* and ask students to look at Side 1. Read the Bible verse aloud. **This Bible verse compares Jesus to the perfect lambs in our story today. In fact, there are lots of similar things between what happened in the Bible story and the good news for us today!** Students complete the diagram, filling in the missing words to show how the Israelites in the Bible story and people today are alike and different.

- ▷ **What does the space in the center of the two circles say?** ("Loved by God." "Need to be rescued.") **These are things that were true for the Israelites, and they are true for us, too!**
- ▷ **How did God rescue the Israelites from slavery in Egypt?** (He sent Moses. He did many miracles.)
- ▷ **How did Jesus rescue us from the penalty for our sin?** (He died on the cross to pay the penalty for our sin. Then He came back to life again.)

Students turn to Side 2 of *Kid Talk Cards*. **God sent Jesus to make the way for us to be forgiven and saved!** Read the prayers aloud and invite students to choose one and then sign their names on their chosen prayers.

- ▷ **Why do you think doing wrong things is a problem?** (We can get in trouble. Sin separates us from God and the good things He wants for us.)
- ▷ Point to photo of cross and invite a student to read aloud the words on the picture. **A cross like this reminds me of how God made it possible for me to become a member of His family—Jesus paid the penalty for my sin!**
- ▷ **Jesus has done many things for us. What's one you want to thank Him for?**

Prayer

Invite volunteers to tell prayer requests as you write them on the whiteboard. Then pray with students about the needs and concerns they mention. Invite students to take turns praying aloud and thanking God for forgiving their sins.

Art

Ahead of time for each student, draw a large open cross shape on a large sheet of construction paper.

Give each student one of the sheets that you prepared. Students use collage materials to fill in the cross shape and decorate the paper.

YOU NEED

Large sheets of construction paper, markers, a variety of collage materials (paper and fabric scraps, ribbon, yarn, etc.), glue sticks.

Connect: **I hope that each time you see a cross, you will remember God's great love for you! He loves you so much that He sent Jesus to make a way to forgive your sin so you could become part of His family!**

TIP

Instead of using glue sticks, provide watered-down white glue and paintbrushes. Students paint glue over cross shape, add collage materials and then paint over the materials with more glue.

Game

Place a container in an open area of your classroom. Tape a large sheet of paper to wall near container.

Students take turns tossing a beanbag into container from different places in the room. On a large sheet of paper write a letter of the word "forgive" each time any student gets the beanbag into the container. Continue until the word is completed. Repeat with the words "God's love" and "saved" as time permits.

YOU NEED

Container, large sheet of paper, tape, beanbags, marker.

Connect: **I am so glad that God made a way for us to be forgiven for the wrong things we have done! Jesus solved our biggest problem: the problem of how to have a relationship with God, even though we have done wrong things.**

Get Going

Direct students to look at Side 2 of their *Kid Talk Cards* again. **As we listen to this song, reread the prayer you signed on your card.** Play "I Will Trust in You" (track 4 on *Worship CD*), inviting students to listen or sing along. **Because God sent Jesus to rescue us, we can trust Him with our lives!** Distribute Lesson 3 *Family Fridge Fun* papers as students leave.

Red Sea Rescue

Dear Teacher,

As I tried to think about times when God has shown His power in my life, I wasn't sure what to write about. I've seen God's kindness, forgiveness and guidance, but I wasn't sure I'd seen the kind of power He showed when He parted the Red Sea!

But I have definitely seen God do GOOD things in my life. When I was angry and hurt by someone I knew, God gave me courage to love that person, and she became one of my best friends. When I was lonely, God taught me that He was enough for me, and I found peace and joy—and I also gained more friends than I'd ever had before! When I couldn't see the plan for my future, God helped me take one step at a time until a whole new path opened up for me.

Wow! God HAS done amazing things for me. I need to praise and thank Him more for His greatness and power!

Becky English
Editor

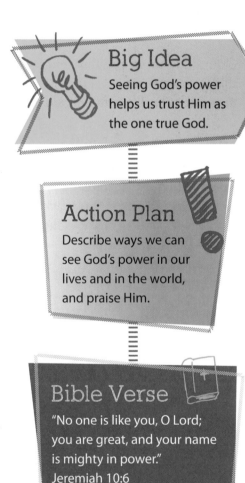

Big Idea

Seeing God's power helps us trust Him as the one true God.

Action Plan

Describe ways we can see God's power in our lives and in the world, and praise Him.

Bible Verse

"No one is like you, O Lord; you are great, and your name is mighty in power."
Jeremiah 10:6

Connecting You to Jesus

The story of the Red Sea crossing gives one picture after another of God's power and His provision for us. By day and by night, God showed His loving care with a pillar of cloud and a pillar of fire. Then when Pharaoh and his soldiers pursued the Israelites, God miraculously rescued the Israelites from certain death. God rescues us from the death we deserve for our sin. He sent Jesus to be the Savior who provides for our every need.

LESSON MATERIALS

- The basics (see contents)
- Toy rocket
- Get Thinking—bowl of water, glitter, toothpick, liquid dish-washing soap
- Story Starter—backpack filled with a variety of travel and other items
- Story props (see p. 39)
- Materials for Art or Game activity (see pp. 44-45)

Lesson Extras!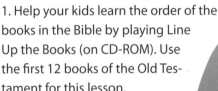

1. Help your kids learn the order of the books in the Bible by playing Line Up the Books (on CD-ROM). Use the first 12 books of the Old Testament for this lesson.

2. Students learn about today's Bible verse by completing Lesson 4 Bible Verse Puzzle (on CD-ROM).

3. DVD Option: Show "Lesson 4: Super Powers" on *Creative Clips DVD*. It's fun to think about having super powers. Super powers are not really real. But today we are talking about real power— God's power!

Get Thinking

Welcome students and help them begin to think about today's Big Idea.

Glitter Scatter

Let's try a fun science experiment! What happens when you add dishwashing soap to a bowl of water and glitter? Add three pinches of glitter to the center of a bowl of water. Ask a volunteer to dip the end of the toothpick in the dishwashing soap and then touch the center of the water with it. **Watch what happens!** Encourage students to discuss how some things are more powerful than others.

Big Idea

Seeing God's power helps us trust Him as the one true God.

YOU NEED

Bowl of water, glitter, toothpick, liquid dishwashing soap.

Connect:

▷ **What happened to the glitter when you touched the soapy toothpick to the water? What do you think made that happen?** (The glitter spread to the edges of the bowl because the soap broke the surface tension of the water.)

▷ **What was more powerful in our experiment— the glitter or the soap? What makes some things more powerful than others?**

▷ **Today we're talking about an amazing event that took a lot more power than soap has!**

Get God's Word (15-25 minutes)

Red Sea Rescue

Tell the following story summary in your own words, asking discussion questions as indicated.

Story Starter

Show backpack. **If you were going to go on a trip, what things would you take with you?** Invite a volunteer to choose two items from the backpack and then decide which of the items he or she would take on a trip. Invite other volunteers to take turns choosing items. Encourage students to have fun with the realistic trip items and the silly ones. **You chose some interesting things to travel with! Going on a trip with all of you could be quite an adventure!** Help students find Exodus 13:21 in their Bibles. Tell students that the first number in the reference is for the chapter and the second number is for the verse. Read Exodus 13:21 aloud. **Let's find out where God was leading the people!**

> ### YOU NEED
>
> Bible for yourself and each student, Lesson 4 Poster, Story Pictures 1-5 (from CD-ROM), backpack filled with a variety of travel and other items (toothbrush, alarm clock, socks, stapler, gift bow, napkin ring, etc.), toy rocket.

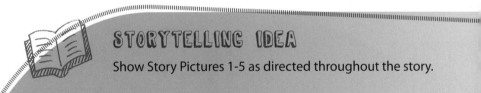

STORYTELLING IDEA

Show Story Pictures 1-5 as directed throughout the story.

Day and Night Protection

The Israelites were off! Pharaoh had FINALLY let them leave Egypt. The people set out on their journey with everything they owned, including their cattle and sheep. God led the people into the desert.

In the daytime, God went ahead of them in a huge, tall cloud that towered over the Israelites and gave them shade in the hot desert. At night, the tall pillar

> ### TIP
>
> Show "Where It All Happened" map on page 40 in *What the Bible Is All About for Kids*, and invite a student to find the Red Sea.

of cloud became a pillar of fire, giving the people light to travel by in the deep darkness and giving them warmth as well. Show Story Picture 1. God never left the people—He stayed with them all the time in the pillar of cloud or the pillar of fire!

Trapped at the Sea

After they had traveled for a little while, God told Moses to have the people camp by the Red Sea. About this time, Pharaoh and his officials decided that they'd made a terrible MISTAKE letting the Israelites leave Egypt! **Listen as I read Exodus 14:5-7 to hear what they did.** Pharaoh and his army got in their chariots and hurried to catch up to the people. It wasn't long before the Israelites heard the distant thunder of thousands of horses' hooves. They looked up from their campsite to see an ARMY coming toward them in the distance!

The Israelites were afraid! They had the sea in front of them, mountains around them and Pharaoh's mighty army behind them. They were trapped! Show Story Picture 2. The people cried to God for help. And then they wailed to Moses, "Didn't we tell you to leave us alone? We'd rather serve the Egyptians than die in the desert!"

"Do not be afraid," Moses told the people. "God will rescue you. You will never see these Egyptians again! God will do the fighting—you just need to be still." Then God told Moses to raise his staff and stretch out his hand over the sea in front of them. God told Moses that He was going to make a path right through the sea and that HE would make sure the Egyptians learned that He is God!

The cloud pillar that had been traveling in front of the people moved BEHIND them. As it got to be nighttime, the pillar became fire so that the Israelites could see. But the side that faced the Egyptians was a thick dark cloud. The Egyptians couldn't see much in the dark. The huge pillar made a safety wall between the Israelites and their enemies.

Moses stretched out his hand over the sea, and all night long, God pushed back the waters of the Red Sea with a strong wind. Show Story

Big Idea

Seeing God's power helps us trust Him as the one true God.

Picture 3. The waters separated and stood up in two high walls, making a path to the other side of the sea! **What do you think the people thought when they saw the path through the sea?**

So the people of Israel went through the sea on dry ground. Show Story Picture 4. But the Egyptians followed the Israelites on the path through the sea, determined to catch them. Suddenly, just before morning, God confused the Egyptian army. He made the wheels of their chariots come off so that it was hard for them to drive! The Egyptians got scared! "Let's get away!" they said. "The Lord is fighting for the Israelites and is against us!"

Then God told Moses to stretch out his hand over the sea again. Moses obeyed, and as the morning sun came up, the sea returned to its place and totally covered Pharaoh and his army. The Israelites were safe! God's power had protected them!

> **TIP**
>
> Show Lesson 4 Poster and ask the students how they think the people might have felt as they walked between the walls of water through the sea.

Songs of Praise

The Israelites were amazed and thankful! God had protected them in a miraculous way! **How do you think the Israelites felt?** They had to CELEBRATE! So Moses and his sister Miriam led the Israelites in singing and dancing before God. Show Story Picture 5. The people created songs on the spot about how God had saved and protected

them! They played tambourines, singing to God and praising Him. The God who could save them from the biggest, strongest, meanest army in the world was CERTAINLY able to bring them to the land He had promised to their fathers!

Wrap-Up

The Israelites were TERRIFIED when they realized they were trapped at the Red Sea. They had nowhere to go—except to God! But they found out that God is the BEST One to trust in times of trouble! Read Jeremiah 10:6 aloud and show toy rocket. **God is so great and so strong that He can handle ANY kind of trouble we face. He is far more powerful than a rocket or any other thing, and He knows how to help us when we have problems or troubles of any kind. He cares about us as much as He cared for the Israelites. God is the only true God, and because of that, we can trust Him. And we can praise and thank Him for His power and His care!**

Action Plan

Describe ways we can see God's power in our lives and in the world, and praise Him.

Connecting Kids to Jesus

The story of the Israelites crossing the Red Sea reminds us again and again of God's power and His care for us. God cared for His people by being with them in a pillar of cloud by day and a pillar of fire by night. When the Israelites were trapped and facing capture by Pharaoh, God rescued them! God cares for us and rescues us, too! God sent His Son, Jesus, to rescue us from the punishment we deserve for our sin.

Get Talking

(25-30 minutes)

Whiteboard Time

On whiteboard, write part of Jeremiah 10:6: "No one is like You, O Lord; you are . . ." **What are some descriptions of God that show He is different from anyone else?** Invite volunteers to suggest different words that describe God ("great," "powerful," "faithful," "eternal," "perfect," etc.). Write words on the whiteboard. **Our verse also says that God's name is "mighty in power."** Tell students that in the Bible, a person's name often told something about who that person was and what he or she was like. **Saying that God's name is mighty and powerful is another way of saying that GOD is mighty and powerful! No one is as great and powerful as God!**

Distribute Lesson 4 *Kid Talk Cards* and ask students to look at Side 1. Read Bible verse aloud. Students match pictures with correct words to see how God showed His power to the Israelites in today's story.

▷ **Why do you think the people did not at first trust in God's power?** (They looked at what was happening and forgot to think about God.)

▷ **What do you think God wanted the Israelites to know about Him?** (That they could trust in Him.)

Students look at Side 2 of *Kid Talk Cards*. Ask students to go through the maze to collect letters and complete the senence about God's power.

▷ **When might you need to trust in God's power?** (When someone tries to hurt me. When I can't understand something at school. When my family is fighting.)

▷ Point to photo of rocket. **Have you ever seen a rocket launch? It takes a LOT of power to send a rocket into space! And God has MUCH more power than that.**

▷ **How does God help people when they are afraid? How does He help when people are lonely?**

▷ **When has God's power helped you?** Be prepared to give an example from your own life. **Praise Him for it!**

Prayer

Invite volunteers to tell prayer requests as you write them on the whiteboard. Then pray with students about the needs and concerns they mention. Ask students to write on sticky notes ways that God shows His power. Post notes on the wall and invite kids to pray with their eyes open, using each others' notes as prompts.

Art

Students use foil, pipe cleaners and toothpicks to create things that remind them of God's power (trees, animals, mountains, people, waterfalls, planets, etc.). Provide glue, tape and scissors for students to use as desired as they create.

> **YOU NEED**
>
> Aluminum foil, pipe cleaners, toothpicks, glue, tape, scissors.

As students work, talk with them about ways that God shows His power in people's personal lives (forgives, comforts, gives courage, etc.) as well as in nature (creates powerful animals, makes huge mountains and plunging waterfalls, keeps the planets in orbit, etc.).

> **TIP**
>
> Take a photo of each student with his or her creation. Ask students to provide captions for their photo, and post photos and captions around the classroom.

Connect: **God cares about us. He loves to show His power in our lives, whether our need is a big one or a little one! Let's praise God for all He does for us every day!**

Game

Ahead of time, blow up and tie balloons.

YOU NEED
Bibles, several balloons, several hardback books.

Invite students to line up, side by side, in an open area of the room. Give each student a balloon. **How many times in a row can you bounce a balloon on your head?** Tell students that they should not touch the balloons with their hands. When you say "Go," students begin bouncing balloons on their heads, counting bounces. Student with the most bounces leads others in repeating the Bible verse. **Let's try another challenge! How far can you walk with a book balanced on your head?** Ask students to line up again. Give each one a book and ask students to balance books on their heads. When you say "Go," students try to walk to the other side of the room and back without touching the book with their hands. If a student touches the book with their hands or a book falls to the floor, student stops walking, rebalances the book and continues to walk. First student back to the starting point leads others in repeating the Bible verse.

Connect: **It can be fun to try challenges! Sometimes we face challenges in life that are a lot harder to handle than bouncing a balloon or balancing a book. But God will help us. We can trust His power!**

Get Going

Direct students to look at Side 2 of their *Kid Talk Cards* again. **God wants to show His power in EVERY area of your lives! He knows exactly what you need in each situation!** Play "My God Will Meet All Your Needs" (track 5 on *Worship CD*), inviting students to listen or sing along. **This week let's remember to trust God and ask for His help with every need, big or little!** Distribute Lesson 4 *Family Fridge Fun* papers as students leave.

OCT.

Food from the Sky

Dear Teacher,

How often do you catch yourself complaining? I have to admit that I find myself complaining much more often than I'd like to! I know my complaints are foolish: "I don't have anything to wear"—but I have a full closet. "I don't have a lot money"—but I have what I need this month. And the list can go on and on.

So how do I stop complaining? It's simple! I think about the amazing ways God has met my needs in the past (a phone call from a friend at just the right moment, an opportunity to earn just the right amount of extra income, a big donation that came out of the blue for a ministry I lead). Or I can simply focus on who God is and what He has done for me! How can I possibly complain when the Creator of the universe loves me so much that He sent His Son to give me eternal life with Him? The only appropriate response is to "give thanks to the Lord for his unfailing love"!

Debbie Barber
Senior Editor

Big Idea

God provides for me, even when I don't recognize His help.

Action Plan

Talk about reasons kids complain, and choose to trust God for my needs.

Bible Verse

"Give thanks to the Lord . . . , for he satisfies the thirsty and fills the hungry with good things." Psalm 107:8-9

Connecting You to Jesus

God provided food and water for the Israelites in the middle of a hostile desert, even though they complained and didn't trust Him. This provision was one of the great signs that Israel's God was the true God, the Lord of creation. Jesus called Himself "the true bread from heaven" (see John 6:32). Through Jesus, God truly meets our greatest needs—our need for forgiveness and the abundant life that only comes through relationship with Him.

LESSON MATERIALS

- The basics (see contents)
- Rock
- Story Starter—unusual-looking food item
- Story props (see p. 49)
- Materials for Art or Game activity (see pp. 54-55)

Lesson Extras!

1. Help your kids learn the order of books in the Bible by playing Go Fish! (on CD-ROM). Use the first 12 books of the Old Testament for this lesson.

2. Students discover what God wanted the people in today's Bible story to learn by completing Lesson 5 Bible Story Puzzle (on CD-ROM).

3. DVD Option: Show "Lesson 5: The Complaininator" on *Creative Clips DVD*. **Pretending to complain can be fun. But in real life, complaining can cause big problems! The Israelites in our story today found out about that!**

Get Thinking

Welcome students and help them begin to think about today's Big Idea.

What Do I Need?

Cover table with butcher paper and use a marker to divide butcher paper into four sections. Print these words in separate sections: "Cold," "Hungry," "Tired" and "Lonely."

In the different sections of the paper, students draw pictures of things that would help them if they had the need written in that section (coat, food, pillow, friend, etc.).

Big Idea

God provides for me, even when I don't recognize His help.

YOU NEED

Butcher paper, markers.

Connect:

- How do you think someone would feel if he or she didn't have one of the things you drew?

- What are some things that people don't REALLY need but complain about not having? (Cool clothes, snack foods, etc.)

- Today we are going to be talking about what God did when some people complained about not having what they needed.

Get God's Word (15-25 minutes)

Food from the Sky

Tell the following story summary in your own words, asking discussion questions as indicated.

Story Starter

Show an unusual-looking food item and begin talking about how much you enjoy eating it, but do not tell students what it is. Continue telling about it, attempting to get students to ask, "What is it?" (Note: Ahead of time, ask a helper to ask the question if students do not ask after a few moments.) Tell students what the food item is. **In our story today, some people asked this very question when they saw some unusual food. You can find out who these people were by reading Exodus 16:1.** Help students find Exodus 16:1 in their Bibles and point to the word "Israelite." **Let's find out about the unusual food the Israelites had.**

YOU NEED

Bible for yourself and each student, Lesson 5 Poster, unusual-looking food item (ethnic food or vegetable with which students are not familiar), story props (see below), rock.

STORYTELLING IDEA

Gather crackers, a can of chicken, a napkin, a pitcher of water and small paper cups. Show and distribute items as directed during story.

A Hungry Crowd

Show crackers, can of chicken and pitcher of water. The Israelites had been out in the desert for about a month after escaping from Egypt. Most of their food supplies had probably been used up. Cover crackers and can of chicken with napkin. **Can you guess what they did? The** people started to complain! "Moses, you made us come out here in the hot desert. It was better when we were slaves in Egypt!"

God heard what the people said. And He told Moses what He was going to do. You see, when the people grumbled, they weren't really complaining about Moses and Aaron. They were complaining about God Himself. They were accusing God of NOT being good and of NOT providing what they needed! Uh-oh!

Food from the Sky

Moses called the people together to tell them what God had said. **Listen as I read Exodus 16:6-7 to hear what Moses told the people.** God wanted the Israelites to know that He is the Lord, that He is good and that He provides what is needed!

TIP

Show Lesson 5 Poster and ask students to tell what they think the kid in the picture is saying.

That evening, a huge flock of birds called quail landed in the camp. There were so many birds that the people could easily catch all they wanted to cook and eat! Show can of chicken.

Then in the morning, the people spotted little flakes of something tasty and sweet all over the ground. The people asked, "What is it?" Show crackers.

Moses said, "This is the bread God has given you!"

Give each student a cracker to eat. The people called this bread "manna," a word that means "What is it?" They could gather all the manna they needed! No matter how many people there were to feed, there was always enough for each day. But if the people tried to save manna overnight, it got stinky and full of mag-

Big Idea

God provides for me, even when I don't recognize His help.

gots! Encourage students to finish eating crackers. God wanted them to trust Him for food every day.

But God told them that on the sixth day of every week, they should gather enough manna for two days. That way, they wouldn't have to go out and gather food on the Sabbath. God was making it possible for His people to rest one day every week and not have to gather food! God made it VERY clear that whatever His people needed, He was able to provide! Give each student two more crackers to eat.

A Thirsty Crowd

Now you would think that with all this amazing food, God's people would remember how God had helped them and be thankful! But then they realized that they were running out of water. Cover water pitcher with napkin. So guess what they did—again! Yes, these people were excellent complainers!

What do you think Moses did? Moses knew that when there was a problem, there was only ONE thing to do—talk to God! And of course, God had a solution. He told Moses to get some of the leaders and walk to a rock that He would direct them to.

Moses raised his staff and hit the rock HARD! And just as God had told him would happen, water GUSHED out of the rock! There was plenty for everyone to drink! Pour a small amount of water in a cup for each student.

> ### TIP
>
> Read aloud "God's Plan for You" on page 36 in *What the Bible Is All About for Kids*, and explain that each child is a part of God's plan!

Wrap-Up

When we have problems or don't have the things we need, sometimes we forget the ways God has already helped us; and instead of being thankful, we complain. But God takes care of us like He took care of the people in our story today, even though they complained and didn't trust Him.

Show rock. **God made water come out of a rock to give the people the water they needed! And today, we can trust God to take care of all our needs, too!** Read Psalm 107:8-9 aloud. **Whenever we feel worried or we want to complain, we can follow Moses' example and talk to God about how we feel and what we need. Because we can't see God, it might be hard for us to remember** that He is real and cares for us. When we see a rock, we can remember that God loves us, that He wants to hear from us and that He will give us what is best for us—sometimes in surprising ways!

Action Plan

Talk about reasons kids complain, and choose to trust God for my needs.

Connecting Kids to Jesus

God gave the hungry and thirsty Israelites the food and water they needed! God showed them that He really is the one true God, the creator of heaven and earth. In the New Testament, Jesus called Himself "the true bread from heaven." When Jesus said that, He was telling people that He was the One who would meet everyone's needs. And that's just what Jesus did when He died on the cross and came back to life again. He made it possible for us to be forgiven and to live as part of God's family!

 **(25-30 minutes)**

Whiteboard Time

On whiteboard, write keywords or phrases from Psalm 107:8-9 in random order ("thirsty," "satisfies," "thanks," "hungry," "good things"). Students take turns telling if the word or phrase describes God or people and writing *G* or *P* next to each word or phrase. Read verse aloud to students. **What does this verse tell us to do?**

Distribute Lesson 5 *Kid Talk Cards* and lead students in reading the Bible verse on Side 1 aloud. **If the Israelites in our story had obeyed these words, what would they have said and done?** Students draw faces to show their answers to the questions.

▷ **Do you think the Israelites trusted God to care for them? Why or why not?**

▷ **What did the Israelites do when they felt that God was not providing for them?** (They complained.) **What did Moses do that was different from the other Israelites?**

▷ **Why did God help the Israelites?** (He loved them, even though they did not deserve it.)

Students turn to Side 2 of *Kid Talk Cards*. **There are a lot of different things we can do when we feel like complaining!** Read aloud the sentence starter. Then invite students to draw a picture that shows how they would complete the sentence about showing that they trust God.

▷ **When might kids your age feel like complaining?**

▷ **When do you think it is easy to trust God? When is it hard to trust Him?**

▷ Point to photo of rock. **In the Bible story today, God used a rock to give His people the water they needed. It seems strange, but that's what He did! And a rock can remind us now that we can trust God to take care of us, no matter what things look like!**

▷ **What can you do when you feel like complaining?** (Remember the good things I have. Look for ways God has helped me.)

Prayer

Invite volunteers to tell prayer requests as you write them on the whiteboard. Then pray with students about the needs and concerns they mention. Start a prayer journal or take time to look back at one you've already started. **What has God done to help you?** Write down the students' answers and then, as a group, thank Him!

Art

Give each student a sandpaper square. Students use crayons to write "Give thanks!" or "Thank God!" and to draw designs on sandpaper, coloring heavily.

YOU NEED

Ten-inch (25.5-cm) square of sandpaper for each student, crayons.

Connect: **Put your sandpaper reminder somewhere where you can see it during the week. Just like God cared for His people in the desert, I hope that the sandpaper reminder will help you remember to trust God with any problem that you face this week. God's love for you is amazing! He will be with you and help you, no matter what happens!**

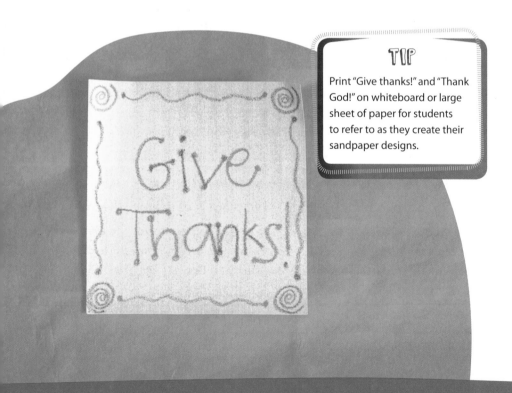

TIP

Print "Give thanks!" and "Thank God!" on whiteboard or large sheet of paper for students to refer to as they create their sandpaper designs.

Game

On one side of an open area, make two piles of one bathrobe and one pair of sandals each. On the other side of the playing area, place a bowl of popcorn and a stack of paper cups across from each pile.

YOU NEED

Two bathrobes, two pairs of adult-sized sandals, two bowls of popped popcorn, small paper cups.

Students form two teams. Each team lines up by one pile of clothing. At your signal, first student in each line quickly puts on cloak (bathrobe) and sandals, walks to basket of "manna" and scoops up one cupful of popcorn. Student then returns to team to give next student in line a turn. After everyone has gathered popcorn, students enjoy eating the popcorn together.

Connect: **God gave the Israelites everything they needed, even though they didn't trust Him and they complained. I hope that you will remember God's love for you when you start to feel like complaining or start to worry about things this week.**

Get Going

Direct students to look at Side 2 of their *Kid Talk Cards* again. **As we listen to this song, think about times this coming week when you might feel like complaining. You can ask God to help you trust Him more and more every day.** Play "My God Will Meet All Your Needs" (track 5 on *Worship CD*), inviting students to listen or sing along. **I'm glad to know that God really will meet all my needs! I can trust God, and I'm going to pray that you will remember to trust God, too!** Distribute Lesson 5 *Family Fridge Fun* papers as students leave.

OCT. 7

Hilltop Battle

Dear Teacher,

One of my favorite heroes of the faith is George Müller. Müller was a pastor who noticed the huge orphan problem in 19th-century Britain and wanted to do something about it. But he also wanted to encourage Christians that God still answers prayer and that "it is not a vain thing to trust in Him." * So Müller started an orphanage and determined never to ask anyone for money. He decided to go only to God with the orphans' needs so people could see "that God is FAITHFUL STILL, and HEARS PRAYER STILL." *

During his lifetime, Müller built five large orphanages and cared for over 10,000 orphans, and he and his staff depended totally on God through prayer. Müller had his faith tested in tough times, but he never quit trusting God, and he had miraculous answers to prayer. What an amazing testimony of how God loves to work through prayer!

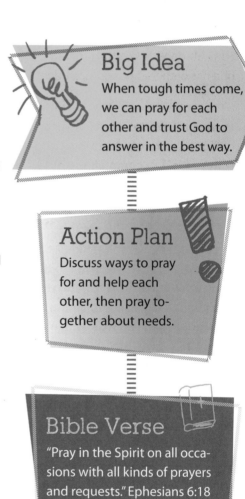

Big Idea

When tough times come, we can pray for each other and trust God to answer in the best way.

Action Plan

Discuss ways to pray for and help each other, then pray together about needs.

Bible Verse

"Pray in the Spirit on all occasions with all kinds of prayers and requests." Ephesians 6:18

Becky English
Editor

* George Müller's Narratives, Vol. 1, Dust and Ashes Publications, http://www.dustandashes.com/434.htm (accessed December 19, 2011).

Connecting You to Jesus

God's help in response to prayer is made clear in the story of the Israelites' defeat of the Amalekites. Moses celebrated the victory by building an altar called "The Lord is my Banner" (Exodus 17:15). The prophet Isaiah later wrote that the Messiah "will stand as a banner for the peoples" (Isaiah 11:10). As long as Moses kept his hands raised in prayer to God, his banner, the Israelites were victorious. The same is true for us: We find salvation and victory only when we look to Jesus!

LESSON MATERIALS

- The basics (see contents)
- Broken toy
- Get Thinking—Legos®
- Story props (see p. 59)
- Materials for Art or Game activity (see pp. 64-65)

Lesson Extras!

1. Help your kids learn the order of books in the Bible by playing Go Fish! (on CD-ROM). Use the first 17 books of the Old Testament for this lesson.

2. Students discover the main idea of the Bible verse by completing Lesson 6 Bible Verse Puzzle (on CD-ROM).

3. DVD Option: **Let's watch this video and see how fast we can memorize Ephesians 6:18.** Show "Lesson 6: Mission Memorization" on *Creative Clips DVD*. **I'm glad we can tell God our problems, no matter what is happening in our lives and no matter how we are feeling!**

Get Thinking  (10-15 minutes)

Welcome students and help them begin to think about today's Big Idea.

Let Me Help You!

Put Legos on table. As students arrive, ask, **What are some things you can think of that help people?** Lead students in talking about different things that help people (cars, tools, books, crutches, etc.), and invite students to build one or more of the suggested objects with Legos.

> ## Big Idea
> When tough times come, we can pray for each other and trust God to answer in the best way.

Connect:

> ### YOU NEED
> Legos®.

▷ **Of all the things our class made, which one do you think might help people most?**

▷ **Why do you think people need help doing things?** (People aren't made to do everything by themselves. God wants us to do things together.)

▷ **Today we'll hear about a man who had a very important job to do that he couldn't do all by himself. But he had some good friends. Let's find out if they were able to help him.**

Get God's Word (15-25 minutes)

Hilltop Battle

Tell the following story summary in your own words, asking discussion questions as indicated.

Story Starter

OK, everybody, I need you to stand up with me! How many arm circles do you think you can do before your arms get too tired to keep going? Put your arms out to your sides, inviting students to follow your actions, and begin counting arm circles aloud. **Can you do 20? How about 40? Or even 50?** Lead students in doing arms circles until you've done 50 or until students' arms are tired. **Phew! Good job! You can sit down now. Are your arms tired? Mine sure are! In today's story, a man's arms got VERY tired, and he needed two of his friends to help him out!** Help students find Exodus 17:11 in their Bibles and point to the words "Moses held up his hands." **Let's listen to find out why Moses was holding up his hands.**

> **YOU NEED**
>
> Bible for yourself and each student, Lesson 6 Poster, broken toy.

STORYTELLING IDEA

Choose three volunteers to play Moses, Aaron and Hur. The other students play the Israelites. As directed throughout story, Aaron and Hur help Moses hold up arms. When Moses' arms are up, Israelites cheer; when his arms are down, Israelites say, "Oh no!"

Under Attack

The Israelites were traveling through the desert, camping at different places where God was leading them. God was also providing food and water for them in amazing ways! The journey was not easy, but the Israelites were learning that God was taking care of them.

But then trouble struck! The Israelites were camped at the place where God had just miraculously given them water out of a rock. Suddenly, an army came and attacked them!

Moses had a helper named Joshua. Joshua was young, but he already loved and obeyed God. Moses was going to need Joshua's help to deal with this army that was attacking the people of Israel!

TIP

Show Lesson 6 Poster and ask students which job they think was most important: the fighting or the praying. Point out that BOTH jobs were needed.

A Battle Plan

"Choose some of our men," Moses told Joshua, "and go out to fight. Tomorrow I will go up the hill with the staff of God in my hands." **Why do you think Moses went up the hill instead of fighting?** Moses knew that his job was to pray!

The next day, Joshua did exactly what Moses had told him to do. He took some of the Israelite men to fight the Amalekite army. Moses went to the top of the hill with his brother Aaron and his friend Hur to pray. Moses raises arms; Aaron and Hur watch. As the fighting began, Moses held up his hands to God. The Israelites began to win! Israelites cheer.

But after a while, Moses lowered his hands. **What do you think happened then?** Moses lowers arms. Suddenly, the Amalekites began to win the battle! Uh-oh! Israelites groan, "Oh no!" So Moses raised his hands to God again. And suddenly, Israel began to win again! Moses raises arms; Israelites cheer. It became very clear that as long as Moses' hands stayed up, the Israelites were winning! Whenever Moses' hands went down, they started to LOSE!

Could you hold up your arms for a whole day? Moses HAD to do it somehow. Keeping his arms up showed that He was trusting in God to help the Israelites in the battle. But it was hard! As the day wore on, Moses got tired. Moses' arms start to droop; Israelites groan. He was going to need some help.

So Aaron and Hur went to work. **How do you think they helped Moses?** They got a large stone for Moses to sit on. Then Aaron stood on one side of Moses and Hur stood on the other. Each of them held up one of Moses' arms! Aaron

Big Idea

When tough times come, we can pray for each other and trust God to answer in the best way.

and Hur hold up Moses' arms; Israelites cheer. Now Moses could keep his hands held high.

Aaron and Hur helped Moses ALL DAY LONG! They must have been very strong men with a LOT of patience! But they knew that if the Israelites were going to win, they had to help Moses keep his hands up in the air, praying. So they did not give up.

A Victory to Remember

With Moses' hands up, Joshua and his men kept fighting all day long. Finally, at sunset, the last Amalekite was defeated. Israel won the battle! Moses, Aaron, Hur and the Israelites cheer loudly.

But it wasn't the Israelites' great fighting that won the battle. No! God gave Israel the victory because Moses, with the help of his friends, kept his hands lifted up to God and kept trusting in Him.

After the battle, God told Moses to write down the story of the victory and to make sure Joshua heard what was written. **Why do you think God wanted Moses to write about the battle?** Someday, after Moses died, Joshua would lead Israel. God wanted Joshua to trust Him always!

To celebrate the victory and to thank God for His help, Moses built an altar out of stones. Then he gave the altar a name! He called it The Lord is my Banner. A banner is something people

> ### TIP
> Read aloud the definition of the word "altar" on page 293 in *What the Bible Is All About for Kids*.

hold up high to show what team they belong to. By giving the altar that name, Moses was helping the Israelites remember that they belonged to God. The victory they had won together was GOD'S victory!

Wrap-Up

Being attacked by the Amalekites was a hard thing for Moses and all the Israelites to go through! We all go through times when things are tough. Show broken toy. Maybe our favorite toy breaks or a friend is mean to us or we have trouble in our families. During times like that, we need to remember that God is the only One who knows the BEST way to help us!

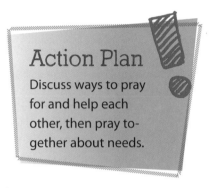

Action Plan

Discuss ways to pray for and help each other, then pray together about needs.

Read Ephesians 6:18. God wants us to pray to Him in our tough situations, like Moses did, and never give up! But sometimes, when life get REALLY hard, we need help even to pray! We need friends who will help us, like Aaron and Hur helped Moses. And not only do we NEED friends, but we can also BE friends to other people who are going through hard times! It is good for us to help each other by praying and trusting in God.

Connecting Kids to Jesus

When Moses held up his hands on the hillside, he was praying and showing that the Israelites were depending on God's help. It was as if he were holding up a banner that said God was winning the battle for everyone to see. In the same way that Moses prayed to and trusted God for victory, we can pray to Jesus and trust Him to save us.

 **(25-30 minutes)**

Whiteboard Time

Print the first phrase of Ephesians 6:18 ("Pray in the Spirit") on the whiteboard. **"Pray in the Spirit" means to pray with God's help for the things God wants us to have. So when do we do that? The rest of the verse tells us when.** Then print the next phrase on the whiteboard ("on all occasions") and invite students to tell how they would say the phrase in their own words ("all the time," "in everything that happens," "whenever," etc.). Then repeat with the remaining phrases. **God wants us to pray to Him all the time, for any need!**

Distribute Lesson 6 *Kid Talk Cards* and read verse on Side 1 aloud. Students complete the dot-to-dot to see how Moses prayed when the Israelites were in trouble.

➢ **When the Israelites were attacked, what two things did Moses do?** (Told Joshua to fight. Went up to pray.)

➢ **How did Moses' friends help him to keep praying?** (They held up Moses' arms when he was tired.)

➢ **How do we know that prayer was the most important job that day?** (Whenever Moses' hands went down, the Israelites started losing the battle.)

Students look at Side 2 of *Kid Talk Cards*. Students write the name of a friend who has a need, draw a picture of the friend and complete the prayer starter by asking God to help the friend.

➢ Point to photo of broken toy. **When have you needed help with a problem? How did you get the help you needed?**

➢ **Think of a friend or family member who needs help with a problem in his or her life right now. How might you help that person?**

➢ **What do you know about God that makes you want to pray to Him?**

➢ **What are some ways we can pray?** (Thank God for what He has given, ask God for help, ask God for forgiveness, tell God how great He is, etc.)

Prayer

Invite volunteers to tell prayer requests as you write them on the whiteboard. Then pray with students about the needs and concerns they mention. Give students a brief time for silent prayer. Encourage them to pray for someone they know who has a need in his or her life.

Art

Give each student a sheet of paper. Students fold paper in half and then fold it in half again to make small booklets. On the front, help students write "_____'s Prayer Book." On each of the other three pages, students draw a picture and/or write the name of a friend or family member they want to pray for. Encourage students to use the booklets this week as a reminder to help others by praying for them.

Connect: **Sometimes I'm not sure how to help a friend, but I know I can always pray for my friend. God knows exactly what our friends need, and He can help them better than anyone else can!**

TIP

If time in class is limited, pre-fold papers and print "_____'s Prayer Book" on each one ahead of time.

Game

Divide class into two or more teams. Students on each team form pairs (partner with a student if needed). Give the first pair on each team a ball. **Your challenge is to get across the room and back with the ball, but you can't move when you are holding the ball!** One student in each pair takes a large step forward. Other student bounces ball to him or her and then also takes a large step forward. Students continue stepping and bouncing ball to move across the room and back. Then students give ball to the next pair in line. First team to get all their pairs across the room and back repeats the Bible verse aloud together. Repeat relay as time allows, forming new teams and pairs.

YOU NEED

Bibles, playground balls.

Connect: **We can help each other when we're playing a game, like we did today, but we can also help each other in real life. A great way to help others is to pray for them!**

Get Going

Direct students to look at Side 2 of their *Kid Talk Cards* again. **It's good to know that God hears our prayers and wants to help us and the people we pray for!** Play "My God Will Meet All Your Needs" (track 5 on *Worship CD*), inviting students to listen or sing along. **I will pray for you this week and ask God to give you everything you need. You can pray for me, too!** Distribute Lesson 6 *Family Fridge Fun* papers as students leave.

God's Top Ten

Dear Teacher,

When you hear the word "law," what is your first reaction? Fear? Discomfort? Or is it gratefulness for God's great love? I know for me, sometimes laws and rules don't feel like love. But the more I learn about God and grow in relationship with Him, the more I understand that God's laws safeguard those He loves.

I think of times when my loved ones or I have come face to face with the painful repercussions of each other's sin. At those times it is all too clear that God has created laws to protect His children, not to condemn them.

Thank God that through His laws we are able to honor and love Him and better love each other. God guides us through His law and frees us through Christ. Now THAT'S a loving God!

Kristina Fucci

Editorial Assistant

Big Idea

God gave us His laws to lead us to Jesus and help us follow Him.

Action Plan

Identify ways we can love God and others every day.

Bible Verse

"Love the Lord your God with all your heart and with all your soul and with all your mind and with all your strength.... Love your neighbor as yourself."
Mark 12:30-31

Connecting You to Jesus

When God gave Moses the Ten Commandments on Mount Sinai, He was showing them
the best way to love Him and others. God's
laws show us how much we need a Savior.
Centuries later, another act of love occurred
on Calvary: Jesus Christ was crucified to pay
the price for our sin! Jesus is the fulfillment of
the Law, and through accepting Him as Savior, we've done all we need to do to receive
forgiveness and salvation.

LESSON MATERIALS

- The basics (see contents)
- Soccer ball
- Get Thinking—a variety of
  board games
- Story props (see p. 69)
- Materials for Art or Game
  activity (see pp. 74-75)

Lesson Extras!

1. Help your kids learn the order of books
in the Bible by playing Go Fish! (on CD-
ROM). Use the first 17 books of the
Old Testament for this lesson.

2. Students talk
about today's
Bible story as
they complete
Lesson 7 Bible
Story Coloring
Page (on CD-ROM).

3. DVD Option:
Show "Lesson 7: Crazy Laws" on
Creative Clips DVD. **There were some
crazy laws in there! But today we are
talking about some laws God gave
us. These laws are really important—and really great!**

Get Thinking (10-15 minutes)

Welcome students and help them begin to think about today's Big Idea.

Play by the Rules!

Place two or more board games with instructions on table. Talk with students about the rules of the games and then invite students to play the games of their choosing together.

Big Idea

God gave us His laws to lead us to Jesus and help us follow Him.

Connect:

> **What are some rules you followed as you played the games?**

> **How much fun would everyone have had if someone kept breaking the rules of the game? How do you think rules help people?** (Rules help to make games fair. People don't get angry with each other as much when things are fair. You can have more fun playing the game.)

YOU NEED

A variety of board games (checkers, Candyland, etc.).

> **Today we are going to find out about some rules God gave us and why He gave them.**

Get God's Word (15-25 minutes)

God's Top Ten

Tell the following story summary in your own words, asking discussion questions as indicated.

Story Starter

What do you need to do to get ready for a birthday party? (Buy a present. Get a card. Clean the house.) **What other kinds of special events do you and your family get ready for?** (First day of school. Christmas. Visit from grandparents.) **What do you do to get ready for these events? A long time ago, in Bible times, Moses and the Israelites had to get ready for a VERY special event. You can find out when it happened by reading Exodus 19:1.** Help students find Exodus 19:1 in their Bibles and follow along as you read the verse aloud. **We'll find out what was going to happen and how the Israelites got ready for it!**

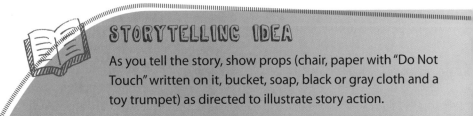

STORYTELLING IDEA

As you tell the story, show props (chair, paper with "Do Not Touch" written on it, bucket, soap, black or gray cloth and a toy trumpet) as directed to illustrate story action.

The Mountain

The Israelites set up their tents to camp at the base of Mount Sinai. They had NO idea what was going to happen next! Place a chair in front of storytelling area to represent the mountain.

Once the people were settled, God called Moses to the top of the moun-

TIP

Read aloud "God's People Camp at Mount Sinai" on page 38 in *What the Bible Is All About for Kids*.

tain and told him how much He loved the Israelites and wanted them to be His special people. He wanted the people to obey His commands. God told Moses what He was going to do next and what to tell the people to do to get ready for the special event.

The Message

Moses went back down the mountain and brought the leaders together. He told everyone what God had said to do, and ALL the people responded together, "We will do everything the Lord has said."

Moses warned the people that God said the mountain was holy. That means it was set apart as a very special place. The people needed to get ready to be near this special place! Place "Do Not Touch" sign on chair.

So for three days, the people washed their clothes and got clean and ready. Show bucket and soap and pretend to wash hands.

On the third day, the mountain was covered in a thick cloud. Place black or gray cloth over chair. Lightning flashed out of the cloud and thunder rumbled, along with the sound of a huge trumpet! Show toy trumpet. WOW! The people began to tremble!

The people stood at the base of the mountain to listen to what God would tell them. **Listen as I read Exodus 20:1-4 to find out what God said first.** These commandments came from God's heart full of love. God wanted these people to love Him and be loyal to Him!

God told Moses that as a way to honor Him, people were not to misuse His name. As another way to honor Him, they were to rest on the seventh day, remembering that God created the world.

Big Idea

God gave us His laws to lead us to Jesus and help us follow Him.

Then God gave commands about honoring others. The fifth commandment said to honor your parents, or show respect to them—and God promised long life to people who did this! **What are some ways kids show respect to their parents?**

The next commandments were to honor others by not killing them, not stealing their wives or husbands, not stealing their things and not lying about them. **Why do you think these are good commands to obey?**

God's last commandment was "Don't covet." "Covet" means to see what someone else has and not just think it's cool but to want it so much that you begin to think of ways to get it! When we obey God's command not to covet, we honor the fact that God is good and has given us good things. When we're not thankful for what we have and want more, we not only dishonor God but also make lots of trouble!

The People's Response

After the people heard the Ten Commandments, they were still trembling with fear. But Moses said, "Don't be afraid! Everything God has said and done today will help you keep from disobeying Him!"

TIP

Show Lesson 7 Poster and ask students to describe what is happening in the picture.

Wrap-Up

God loved the Israelites so much that He wanted to help them be happy and safe! So the first four commandments told the Israelites how to show love to God. The last six commandments helped the Israelites know how to show love to each other.

God loves us just as much as He loved the Israelites. Because of this, He wants to help and protect us, too! And even more important, God's laws show us how much we need Jesus to be our Savior. Here's how Jesus described God's laws. Read Mark 12:30-31 aloud. **Jesus said that we need to love God with our whole lives and that we need to love each other, too!** Show soccer ball. **Just like we need rules to help us play soccer, we need God's laws to help us in our lives. God's rules not only protect us, but they also protect those around us. When we obey God, He helps us to show love to Him and other people!**

Action Plan

Identify ways we can love God and others every day.

Connecting You to Jesus

God gave Moses and the Israelites the Ten Commandments to show them the best way to love Him and love each other. Sometimes when people hear the word "law," they think it means they have to be perfect. God knows we can't be perfect—that's why He sent Jesus! God's laws show us how much we need Jesus as our Savior. Talk with interested students about becoming members of God's family (see "Connecting Kids to Jesus" on pp. 3-5).

Get Talking **(25-30 minutes)**

Whiteboard Time

Read Mark 12:30-31 aloud, stopping after the word "heart" and inviting a student to draw a heart in the center of the whiteboard. Continue reading, stopping after "soul" and drawing a body around the heart (minus head and arms). Continue, drawing a head for "mind" and arms for "strength" and then another person for "neighbor." **God wants us to love Him with our whole lives, showing love for Him in the things we do, say and think about. And one of the great ways to show our love for God is to show His love to other people!**

Distribute Lesson 7 *Kid Talk Cards*. **Let's see how the commandments God gave us match what our Bible verse says.** As you read each command aloud, students draw lines to match the command to either "God" or "Others."

▷ **Why did God give the Ten Commandments?** (To show us how much we need Jesus as our Savior. To tell His people the best way to live. To show His love.)

▷ **Which of the commandments tell us ways to love God? Which tell us ways to love others?**

▷ **What did the people say they would do after they heard God's commandments?** (They would obey them.)

Students turn to Side 2 of *Kid Talk Cards*. **Following God's commands will help you show love to Him and to others!** Students write or draw in the spaces ways to show love to those shown in the outlines.

▷ **What are some things that happen when people don't obey God's commands to treat other people well?** (People get angry or hurt. They fight.)

▷ Point to photo of soccer ball and invite a student to read aloud the words on the picture. **What do God's rules help us know?**

Prayer

Invite volunteers to tell prayer requests as you write them on the whiteboard. Then pray with students about the needs and concerns they mention. **What do you think a kid would say is the hardest commandment to keep?** Pray once again, asking God's help to obey the commands kids mentioned and thanking Jesus for forgiveness when we sin.

Art

Give each student a Verse Chain sheet. Students cut apart strips and decorate the strips. On blank strips, students write or draw pictures of things they can do to show love to others (help, share, etc.) or to show love to God (pray, sing, etc.). Help students make loops with the strips, taping them together in verse order to make a chain, adding the extra strips as desired.

Connect: **Your chains have some great ways of showing love to God and others! I hope that you will put your chain in a place where you will see it and remember to love God in every part of your life and in everything you do!**

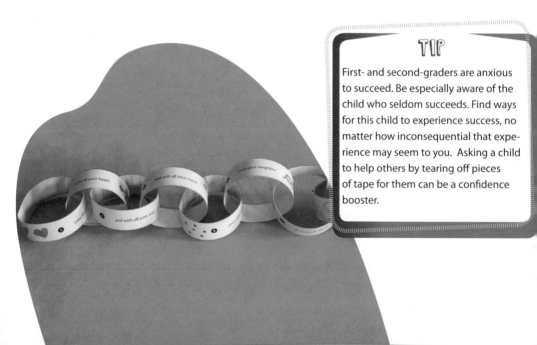

TIP

First- and second-graders are anxious to succeed. Be especially aware of the child who seldom succeeds. Find ways for this child to experience success, no matter how inconsequential that experience may seem to you. Asking a child to help others by tearing off pieces of tape for them can be a confidence booster.

Game

Print the words of Mark 12:30-31 on index cards, three to four words on a card. Make one set of verse cards for every 8 to 10 students.

YOU NEED

Bibles, index cards, marker.

Group students in teams of no more than 8 to 10. Each team lines up on one side of an open area. Students remove shoes and socks. Place a mixed-up set of verse cards across the open area from each team. At your signal, first student on each team skips across to cards, picks up one card and places it between his or her first two toes. Student walks back to team with card held between toes. If card falls out before he or she returns to the team, student must stop to replace card between toes before continuing. Next student in line repeats action until all cards have been collected. Students on each team work together to put cards in verse order. First team finished reads verse aloud. (Students check verse in Bible as needed.)

Connect: **When we show love to other people and to God, we are obeying God's commands! God loves us so much, and He wants us to show His love to others.**

Get Going

Direct students to look at Side 2 of their *Kid Talk Cards* again. **This week, I hope you remember that God's laws help us show love to others and to Him.** Play "Deep as the Ocean" (track 1 on *Worship CD*), inviting students to listen or sing along. **Who will you show God's love to this week? Let me know what happens next week!** Distribute Lesson 7 *Family Fridge Fun* papers as students leave.

Idol Trouble

Dear Teacher,

When I was eight or nine years old, I went through several tough days when I felt very guilty about something I'd done. It was terrible! I didn't want to tell anyone what I'd done, but I sure felt awful keeping quiet. Finally, I couldn't stand it anymore, and I poured the whole mess out to my mom one night as she was tucking me into bed. And you know what? My guilt was suddenly gone! My mom forgave me, and she helped me confess my sin to God. I was so glad that I'd finally told someone my problem.

It can be hard to talk about sin sometimes, but what kid hasn't experienced the weight of a guilty conscience? And what child wouldn't be glad to know that Jesus wants to forgive us and make us clean? I'm so glad to have the privilege of telling kids that good news now that I'm all grown up and still depending on God's forgiveness and grace.

Becky English
Editor

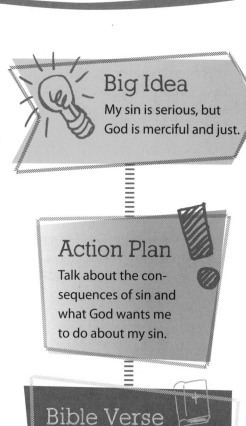

Big Idea

My sin is serious, but God is merciful and just.

Action Plan

Talk about the consequences of sin and what God wants me to do about my sin.

Bible Verse

"If we confess our sins, he is faithful and just and will forgive us our sins and purify us from all unrighteousness."
1 John 1:9

Connecting You to Jesus

Moses urgently interceded for the people of Israel after they sinned by making and worshiping an idol. Moses even asked God to let the punishment for their sin fall on him (see Exodus 32:32). His offer was refused because each person must face the penalty for his or her own sin—and that penalty is death. But God did not leave His people without hope! He sent His one and only Son, Jesus Christ, to make atonement for all people so He could truly forgive our sin.

LESSON MATERIALS

- The basics (see contents)
- Road sign
- Get Thinking—Waiting Games Instructions (from CD-ROM), paper, pens or pencils, pennies
- Story props (see p. 79)
- Materials for Art or Game activity (see pp. 84-85)

Lesson Extras!

1. Help your kids learn the order of books in the Bible by playing Go Fish! (on CD-ROM). Use the first 22 books in the Old Testament for this lesson.

2. Students talk about today's Bible verse as they complete Lesson 8 Bible Verse Coloring Page (on CD-ROM).

3. DVD Option: **Here's a game where you really have to pay attention and concentrate on what is happening. Show** "Lesson 8: Flashback Memory" on *Creative Clips DVD*. **Today we are going to talk about something that is REALLY important to pay attention to!**

Get Thinking

Welcome students and help them begin to think about today's Big Idea.

Waiting Games

Ahead of time, cut apart Waiting Games Instructions and place instructions, paper, pens or pencils and pennies on table.

Big Idea

My sin is serious, but God is merciful and just.

Do you ever play games while you're waiting for something? As students arrive, invite them to play simple games that people often occupy themselves with while waiting for something (at a restaurant, in the doctor's office, while traveling, etc.). Students move from game to game as they desire and as time allows.

YOU NEED

Waiting Games Instructions (from CD-ROM), scissors, paper, pens or pencils, three pennies.

Connect:

▷ **Do you ever play these games when you're waiting for something? Other games?**

▷ **Besides playing games, what are some other things people do when they are waiting? Why do you think people like to keep busy while waiting?** (To keep from getting bored. To stay out of trouble.)

▷ **Today we're going to hear about some people who got impatient while waiting for someone, and they got into really big trouble!**

Get God's Word (15-25 minutes)

Idol Trouble

Tell the following story summary in your own words, asking discussion questions as indicated.

Story Starter

Have you ever had to wait a LONG time for some-thing? Was it hard to be patient? Tell students about a time when you had to wait for something and got into trouble while you were waiting (it could be a funny experience you had as a kid or a more serious situation that had bigger consequences). **Waiting can be hard sometimes, and getting impatient can lead to trouble!** Help students find Exodus 24:14 in their Bibles and find the word "Wait." **Let's find out what the Israelites did while they were waiting for Moses, and the BIG trouble it got them into.**

STORYTELLING IDEA

Ask an adult volunteer to whisper responses from Story Responses sheet to different students as directed throughout story. Students state responses aloud.

Awed by God

It was an important day for the Israelites! Moses was telling them the laws God gave them as His very own people. Everyone listened carefully as Moses talked. When he was finished, everyone called out: Student repeats Story Response 1.

The next morning, Moses again told God's laws to the people, and again the people said: Student repeats Story Response 2.

> **YOU NEED**
>
> Bible for yourself and each student, Lesson 8 Poster, Story Responses sheet (from CD-ROM), road sign.

> **TIP**
>
> Show "When Events Happened" timeline on page 36 in *What the Bible Is All About for Kids* and remind students of the first four events pictured.

Soon after this, God told Moses to come back up the mountain. God wanted to write His laws on tablets of stone and give them to Moses. So Moses told his brother, Aaron, to look after the people while he was gone. When Moses got to the top of the mountain, God covered it with a cloud. To the Israelites down below, the top of the mountain looked like a huge fire! Moses stayed on the mountaintop, hidden in the cloud, for 40 days.

Tired of Waiting

The people waited and waited. And then they waited some more! But after a while, they thought Moses was taking WAY too long. So did the people pray? No. Did they think about God's laws? NO! **What do you think the people did?** They went to Aaron and said: Two students repeat Story Responses 3 and 4. They wanted Aaron to make them an IDOL! Wait. **What were God's first two commandments?** Have NO other gods, and do NOT make idols or bow to them!

Aaron knew better, but he decided to disobey God's laws, too. So he told the Israelites to bring him their gold earrings. Aaron melted the earrings down and formed the gold into the shape of a CALF—a baby cow. The Israelites were delighted! They said: Student repeats Story Response 5. How silly was that?!

Aaron saw how PLEASED the people were! The next morning, Aaron led the people in making offerings to the calf. Then they had a huge, wild PARTY! **What do you think God thought of the people's actions?**

Troubled by Truth

God was not happy! Moses was up on the mountain with God, so God told him, "Go back down there! Those people have already broken My laws! They've made an idol and worshiped it!"

Moses hurried down the mountain, holding the two stone tablets that God had given him. Moses could hear party

Big Idea
My sin is serious, but
God is merciful and just.

noises from far away! When Moses got close enough to see what was going on, he THREW down the stone tablets that God had written on with His own hand, and they shattered! The people had broken their promise to God!

Moses destroyed the idol. Then Moses turned to Aaron and asked: Student repeats Story Response 6. **What do you think Aaron said?** Two students repeat Story Responses 7 and 8. Can you believe it? Aaron blamed the PEOPLE, and then he LIED!

> **TIP**
>
> Show Lesson 8 Poster and ask students why they think Moses was so angry with the Israelites.

Moses knew the Israelites' sin was very serious. So he went back to talk to God. He begged God to forgive the people for their sin. He even asked God to punish him instead. What a mess! God loved the Israelites, but something HAD to be done! Some of the people died. And God told the people that He would not go with them to the Promised Land.

The people were VERY sorry. Moses prayed again, asking God: Student repeats Story Response 9. God told Moses to carve two new stone tablets and to come back up the mountain so He could write the laws again.

"I am kind and good," He told Moses, "and I forgive wickedness and sin." God told Moses that He would go with them. Even though the people's sin had been very great, God was merciful and forgiving.

Wrap-Up

The Israelites didn't keep their promise to obey God's laws for very long at all! But all of us act like that sometimes. We do wrong things even when we know what is right. God takes it seriously when His people sin, because He knows that sin will destroy us. But He is also merciful. Show road sign. **Just like road signs give us directions, God tells us what we can do when we DO sin.** Read aloud 1 John 1:9. **God says that if we admit our sin to God, He will forgive us and wash away our sin. That is something we can be very thankful for!** Talk with interested students about becoming members of God's family (see "Connecting Kids to Jesus" on pp. 3-5).

Action Plan

Talk about the consequences of sin and what God wants me to do about my sin.

Connecting Kids to Jesus

After the people broke God's laws, Moses begged God to forgive them. Moses even asked God to punish him instead! But each person must face the punishment for his or her own sin. The Bible says that the punishment for sin is death. Only Jesus, God's own Son, could pay for people's sin! Jesus died on the cross to take the punishment for all our sin so that we could be forgiven. And Jesus came back to life again! He promises that when we trust in Him, we can be forgiven and live forever with Him.

Get Talking  (25-30 minutes)

Whiteboard Time

On whiteboard, draw one line for each letter of the word "confess." Students guess letters to fill in the blanks as in Hangman. Print wrong letters at the bottom of the board and give hints as needed. When students guess the word, invite volunteers to tell what they think the word means. Repeat with other words in the verse ("faithful," "just" and "purify"). **These words are part of our Bible verse today.** Read 1 John 1:9 aloud. **In other words, this verse says, "If we admit that we have done wrong things, God will forgive us. We can trust God to do this. He always does what is right. He will wash away all our sin."**

Distribute Lesson 8 *Kid Talk Cards*. Students read the statements on Side 1 and then mark each statement as true or false.

▷ **Why did the Israelites make an idol?** (They got impatient. They forgot their promise to obey God's laws.)

▷ **What happened as a result of the wrong things the people did?**

▷ **How did God show the Israelites that He was faithful AND just?** (He punished them for their sin, but He also forgave them and went with them on their journey.)

Students look at Side 2 of *Kid Talk Cards*. Students follow each path in the steps of forgiveness and then fill in the blanks with the words they find on each path.

▷ Point to photo of road sign. **How do road signs help us?** (They give us directions.) **God gives us directions, too! When we have sinned and gotten ourselves into trouble, God wants us to know how we can find forgiveness. He loves us and wants us to be made clean from our sin!**

▷ **When we've disobeyed God, how do we know that He still loves us?** (The Bible tells us that God is ALWAYS willing to forgive us when we admit our wrong.)

▷ **What can we do when we have done something wrong? What does God promise He will do when we confess our sins?**

Prayer

Invite volunteers to tell prayer requests as you write them on the whiteboard. Then pray with students about the needs and concerns they mention. **What are some things we might be tempted to think are more important than loving and obeying God? As I pray again, I will pause so you can silently ask God to help you put Him first.**

Art

Give each student a Steps of Forgiveness Cards sheet. Students color and cut out each card. Students lay each card in order, facedown, beginning with the "Steps of Forgiveness" title card. Give students two lengths of ribbon to lay along the backside of the cards and to tape to each card. Students tie the long ends of ribbons above the title card to make a hanger. Trim ends of ribbon if necessary.

YOU NEED

One Steps of Forgiveness Cards sheet (from CD-ROM) printed on card stock for each student, crayons, scissors, two 30-inch (76-cm) lengths of ribbon for each student, tape.

Connect: **This week when you see your Steps of Forgiveness Hanger, remember how faithful God is to forgive you! He loves you and provides you with a way to fix things when you mess up!**

TIP

Make a sample Steps of Forgiveness Hanger ahead of time for students to see what completed art looks like as they are working. Have ribbon and tape precut and ready for each student.

Game

Ahead of time, crumple aluminum foil to make a small Ping-Pong-sized ball.

Invite students to stand in a circle, and give each student a large plastic cup. Play "My God Will Meet All Your Needs" from *Get Going! Worship CD*. Students toss the foil ball around the circle, catching and tossing the ball with their cups. When the music stops, student with the ball in his or her cup tells one of the steps of forgiveness (confess your sin, ask God for forgiveness, apologize to the person you hurt, thank God that He forgave you, ask God for help to not sin again). Repeat game as time permits.

> **YOU NEED**
>
> *Get Going! Worship CD* and player, aluminum foil, one large plastic cup for each student.

Connect: **God is so loving that even though we sin, He is faithful and just to forgive us! He also tells us what He wants us to do when we sin. When we follow these steps, we know we have made things right with God and with the person we've hurt. And most importantly, we know we're forgiven!**

Get Going

Direct students to look again at Side 2 of their *Kid Talk Cards*. **Aren't you glad that God loves us so much that He wants to forgive us and wash away our sin?** Play "Deep as the Ocean" (track 1 on *Worship CD*), inviting students to listen or sing along. **This week, remember that God's love is deeper than any trouble we could ever get into!** Distribute Lesson 8 *Family Fridge Fun* papers as students leave.

A Perfect Tent

Dear Teacher,

Sometimes I wish for some great talent or skill that would be worthy to offer to God in response to all that He has given me. Other times, I'm like the Israelites on their journey to the Promised Land—I disobey God and doubt His faithfulness. But the building of the Tabernacle was a bright spot in the Israelites' journey—a journey filled with disobedience and doubt! And it reminds me that even when I totally fail in my faith, I still have opportunities for giving my all in worshiping and honoring God.

God knows all my failings—and He made a way to forgive them through Jesus Christ! Because of His forgiveness, God wants even me, a sinner, to give willingly and work diligently to worship and honor Him!

Debbie Barber
Senior Editor

Big Idea
God is so great that I want to honor Him by using my gifts and talents.

Action Plan
Identify ways to honor God by doing what I am good at.

Bible Verse
"You are worthy, our Lord and God, to receive glory and honor and power."
Revelation 4:11

Connecting You to Jesus

When Moses led the Israelites in building the Tabernacle, it was a way of honoring and worshiping their mighty God. But even more than that, the parts of the Tabernacle foreshadowed Jesus and what He came to do. Each detail—especially the lampstand, the laver and the altar—pointed to Jesus as our Savior who would wash away His people's sins by dying on the cross.

LESSON MATERIALS

- The basics (see contents)
- Mirror
- Get Thinking—play dough
- Story props (see p. 89)
- Materials for Art or Game activity (see pp. 94-95)

Lesson Extras!

1. Help your kids learn the order of the books in the Bible by playing Pick and Choose (on CD-ROM). Use the first 22 books of the Old Testament for this lesson.

2. Students talk about the Bible story as they complete Lesson 9 Bible Story Coloring Page (on CD-ROM).

3. DVD Option: **Check out how these kids are using their abilities to honor God.** Show "Lesson 9: Kids Who Serve" on *Creative Clips DVD*. **When we do our best in whatever God has made us able to do, we honor God.**

Get Thinking

Welcome students and help them begin to think about today's Big Idea.

Dough Doings

Students use play dough to make things they use when doing some of their favorite things (soccer ball, game controller, paintbrush, dog leash, etc.). Invite each student to tell others about the object he or she has made.

Big Idea

God is so great that I want to honor Him by using my gifts and talents.

Connect:

YOU NEED

Play dough.

» What are some things you enjoy doing? What have others said you are good at doing?

» What is something you haven't done yet, but you think you would like to try? Why?

» Today we'll find out a great way to use the things we are good at and enjoy doing.

Get God's Word (15-25 minutes)

A Perfect Tent

Tell the following story summary in your own words, asking discussion questions as indicated.

Story Starter

Whisper the word "sawing" to a volunteer or helper. Volunteer or helper pantomimes sawing for students to guess the skill. Give clues as needed. Repeat with other things people might be good at (cooking, painting, sewing, etc.). **There are so many different things that people can do! In our story today, we'll find out why many different people worked together doing the things they were good at. You can find out who wanted the people to do this by looking at Exodus 25:1.** Help students find Exodus 25:1 in their Bibles and point to "the Lord." **Let's find out what happened!**

YOU NEED

Bible for yourself and each student, Lesson 9 Poster, mirror.

STORYTELLING IDEA

Guide students to make motions to show story action as directed throughout story.

God's Plan

Moses and the Israelites had been traveling through the desert on their way to the new land God had promised them. **How did God help the Israelites while they traveled? What had He given them?** (Pillars of cloud and fire to guide them. Food and water. His laws.) When God spoke to Moses, He also gave Moses a very specific plan for something He wanted His people to make. God wanted His people

TIP

Read aloud the definition of "Tabernacle" on page 330 in *What the Bible Is All About for Kids*.

to make a Tabernacle, a special tent with special furniture inside. Every part of it was to be made so that all of it could easily be moved. The Tabernacle would be a place for God's people to worship Him.

Now you might think a tent wouldn't be a very pretty place. But THIS tent would be the most beautiful tent the people had ever seen! **Listen as I read Exodus 35:5-9 to find out why the Tabernacle would be so beautiful. What did Moses tell the people to give?** God wanted the people to give only if they wanted to. No one would be forced to give.

Generous Givers

The list of things needed for the Tabernacle was pretty amazing: special wood, beautiful stones, gold, animal skins and olive oil. The Tabernacle would need colorful fabrics in red, blue and purple, along with many spices!

What do you think the people did? The people began to bring everything that was needed. Students reach hands out as if giving gifts. Then God told Moses that He had given two men, Bezalel and Oholiab, the ability and skills to MAKE everything needed for the Tabernacle. The two men would not only use the skills God had given them but would also teach others how to do this special work so that it could be done quickly!

Soon people were spinning thread and weaving cloth. Men were shaping wood and covering it with gold. Several students pretend to hammer. Others were sewing together the huge pieces of fabric that would become the tent and the fabric walls of the Tabernacle. Several students pretend to sew.

But there was a small problem! The people kept bringing more and more gifts. All students reach hands out as if giving gifts. Soon there was more than was needed! It was a good problem to have! It seems that the people really wanted to give everything they could to make the Tabernacle

Big Idea

God is so great that I want to honor Him by using my gifts and talents.

beautiful! So Moses told everyone to stop bringing materials, because they already had more than enough! **How do you think the people felt?**

God's Presence

The day came when the work was all done. Moses came and checked everything to be sure it was exactly as God had told him to make it. Everything was done well! Moses was glad. So were all the people!

TIP

Show Lesson 9 Poster and invite volunteers to describe the different jobs people are doing in the picture.

Then God told Moses, "On the first day of the first month, set up the Tabernacle." Moses was to set everything up according to the pattern God had shown him. So Moses began his work.

Moses hung the curtains inside the tent. He moved each piece of furniture to its proper place. Then he put up the posts for the outside walls and hung fabric around the courtyard. It was a HUGE job!

When Moses had finished the work, the cloud that had led them all the way COVERED the Tabernacle! Now the people knew that God was with them. From then on, whenever the cloud stopped, the people set up camp, and the cloud covered the Tabernacle. Whenever the cloud lifted from the Tabernacle, the Israelites knew that it was time to move. If the cloud didn't leave the Tabernacle, they didn't leave, either. God was with them, directing them and protecting them in all their travels!

Wrap-Up

The Israelites did their very best work to build a special place for worshiping God. They followed God's instructions exactly, and they did it with a great attitude! They were happy to give to God. The finished Tabernacle was an amazing place! All the things the Israelites willingly gave and the work they willingly did showed how much they wanted to honor God.

Read Revelation 4:11 aloud. **When we do our best in whatever God has made us able to do, we honor God, just like the Israelites did.** Show mirror and turn it so that it catches the light and reflects light upward. **Our lives can be kind of like a mirror. When we honor God and show love to Him by willingly doing the good things God made us able to do, we** shine the light on God like this mirror shines the light. We can also honor God by thanking Him for the things He has given us and the way He helps us as we obey Him.

Action Plan

Identify ways to honor God by doing what I am good at.

Connecting Kids to Jesus

Moses and the Israelites were glad to build the Tabernacle. They loved God and wanted to worship Him! Each part of the Tabernacle reminds us of who Jesus is and what He came to do. Jesus is the Savior who made forgiveness of our sins possible by dying on the cross.

 **(25-30 minutes)**

Whiteboard Time

Down the left side of the whiteboard, print the word "HONOR." **What are some things we do to show that we honor God?** As students tell ideas ("help others," "obey parents," "notice good things God gives," "own up to wrong things you do," "read your Bible," etc.), write them on whiteboard, attaching them to the word "honor" as in an acrostic. Help students with suggestions as needed. **These are just some of the ways we can honor God!**

Distribute Lesson 9 *Kid Talk Cards* and ask students to look at Side 1. Read the Bible verse aloud. **The Israelites knew that God was so great and wonderful that He deserved to be honored and praised! Circle the things the Israelites did, and cross out the things they did NOT do!**

> **What part of the Tabernacle would you have wanted to make? Why?**

> **Why do you think the Israelites were so willing to help build the Tabernacle?**

> **What are some of the ways the Israelites showed that they honored God?**

Students turn to Side 2 of *Kid Talk Cards* and look at the pictures. **How could these kids honor God by doing what they are good at?** Students tell ideas. Then students draw in the space one thing they want to do to honor God.

> Point to the mirror photo and read the words on it aloud. **When light shines on a mirror, the mirror shines the light back. What talents do you have that can shine glory and praise back to God?**

> **What's the difference between doing what you're good at for yourself and doing what you're good at to give honor to God?**

> **How can you honor God when you think you're not good at anything?** (Do my best. Ask God for help.)

Prayer

Invite volunteers to tell prayer requests as you write them on the whiteboard. Then pray with students about the needs and concerns they mention. Read Ephesians 2:10 aloud. Talk about the unique gifts each student has and then ask God to give them wisdom to notice and use their gifts for Him.

Art

Give each student a fabric square and markers to make part of a worship banner. On fabric squares, students complete one of these sentence starters: "God, I really like that You . . ."; "Thank You for . . ."; or "God is . . ." Students glue on additional decorating materials to decorate squares. Create a large worship banner by taping decorated squares together like a quilt. Display banner in your classroom or in a well-traveled area in your church.

Connect: **Our banner shows honor to God! We thanked Him for good things He has done and we praised Him for who He is. This week, I hope that you will remember to talk to God and do your best to honor Him in whatever you do.**

TIPS

1. Simplify project by using paper instead of fabric.

2. To make a permanent worship banner, provide fabric or permanent markers for students to use. Instruct students to leave a small border. After class, give completed squares to a quilter in your church to sew together as a quilt.

Game

Divide group into two equal teams. Teams line up at one end of the room. Place a pile of blocks at the opposite end of the room in a direct line with each team.

YOU NEED

Blocks.

At your signal, the first player in line high-fives the next player in line, who high-fives the next player and so on down the line. After receiving a high five, the last player in line runs to his or her team's blocks and stacks two to start a tower. Player then runs to the front of the line and keeps the motion going by high-fiving the next player in line and so on. Players shift down one position in line as each runner returns. The first team to stack at least 15 blocks to make a tower wins the round. Repeat as time permits. Challenge students to tell three ways to honor God between each round of the game.

Connect: **You thought of some great ways to honor God. Good job! I hope that you will use some of these ideas this week as you do the things you are good at and the things that you enjoy doing. God is worthy of our praise and honor!**

Get Going

Direct students to look at Side 2 of their *Kid Talk Cards* again. **As we listen to this song, talk to God about your plan to honor Him this week.** Play "One True God" (track 6 on *Worship CD*), inviting students to listen or sing along. **We bow and worship God because He is the one true God who is worthy of all our praise!** Distribute Lesson 9 *Family Fridge Fun* papers as students leave.

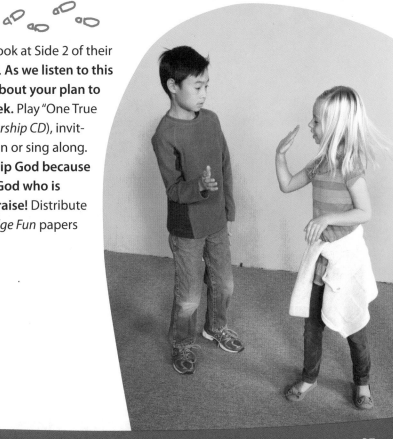

Top-Secret Spies

Dear Teacher,

I don't know about you, but I love the story of Israel's journey to Canaan! Everything about this trek fascinates me: God's provision, the Israelite's disobedience, the thrilling faith of a few choice men! The whole journey can be summarized in the 12 spies' report about the Promised Land—a 10:2 ratio of unbelief to faith!

Sometimes it is hard for me to understand why after EVERYTHING God had done for them, the Israelites still let their fear disqualify them from God's promise! But when I reflect on my life, I wonder, *How often am I like the 10 spies?* God has proven Himself worthy, yet I sometimes doubt His love and provision.

Like the trusting two, I want to step out in faith. Even when those around me fearfully see with their own eyes, I want to faithfully see God's ability to conquer the impossible! Oh, to be like Caleb and Joshua and enter that Promised Land! There IS a spot for you and me, but it requires wholehearted faith. I'll meet YOU there!

Big Idea

Even when others choose not to, I will keep trusting God.

Action Plan

Identify words and actions that show I trust in God.

Bible Verse

"In God I trust; I will not be afraid. What can man do to me?" Psalm 56:11

Kristina Fucci

Editorial Assistant

Connecting You to Jesus

Even when facing giants, Joshua and Caleb trusted in God and had faith in His promises. Joshua's faith points us to Jesus, and so does his name. "Joshua" means "the Lord saves," and the Greek form of the name is "Jesus." Just as Joshua led the people into the Promised Land, Jesus leads all of us—His followers—to salvation and eternal life in heaven.

Lesson Extras!

1. Help your kids learn the order of the books in the Bible by playing Pick and Choose (on CD-ROM). Use the first 22 books of the Old Testament for this lesson.

2. Students talk about today's Bible story as they complete Lesson 10 Bible Story Coloring Page (on CD-ROM).

3. DVD Option: Show "Lesson 10: Trust Me" on *Creative Clips DVD*. **Would you trust that guy? I don't think so! But today we are talking about who we can trust, no matter what situation we are in!**

LESSON MATERIALS

- The basics (see contents)
- Chair
- Get Thinking—several classroom objects, blindfold
- Story Starter—one Scenic Sites Picture (from CD-ROM) for every five students
- Story props (see p. 99)
- Materials for Art or Game activity (see pp. 104-105)

Get Thinking

Welcome students and help them begin to think about today's Big Idea.

Trust Walk!

Ahead of time, set up an obstacle course throughout the room using classroom objects such as desks, chairs, blocks, books, etc.

In pairs, students take turns leading blindfolded partner through obstacle course.

Big Idea

Even when others choose not to, I will keep trusting God.

YOU NEED

Several classroom objects (desks, chairs, blocks, books, etc.), blindfold.

Connect:

▷ **How did you feel going through the obstacle course blindfolded?**

▷ **Why was it so important to listen to your partner's voice and do what he or she said?** (He or she guided me. I couldn't see for myself.)

▷ **Today we're going to hear about a time God promised something BIG! Let's find out if the people listened to God's promise and trusted Him!**

Get God's Word (15-25 minutes)

Top-Secret Spies

Tell the following story summary in your own words, asking discussion questions as indicated.

Story Starter

Divide class into groups of five and give each group a copy of Scenic Sites Picture. **Look at your picture.** Students call out responses to the following questions: **Are there a lot of people or just a few? Where do you think the people are? What kinds of food do you see? Are there any trees? Water? In today's story, we'll find out about a time when God sent people to find the answers to some questions like these! Let's find Numbers 13 in our Bibles to find out where God wanted the Israelites to go to find those answers.** Help students find Numbers 13:1-2 in their Bibles and point to "Canaan." **Let's find out what happened!**

> **YOU NEED**
>
> Bible for yourself and each student, one Scenic Sites Picture (from CD-ROM) for each group of five students, Lesson 10 Poster, spy costume, chair.

STORYTELLING IDEA

Dress in spy costume (trench coat, sunglasses, hat, magnifying glass, etc.) and tell story as if training students to become spies. Ask questions as directed throughout story.

A Spy Mission

Today you'll be spies in training! And we are going to hear a story about some experienced spies as we train! Do you remember Moses and the Israelites? Well, they were camped just outside of Canaan—the land God had promised to give them. It looked like they would be moving into the new land REALLY soon! God told Moses to send 12 spies to explore the land He was giving them. Spies are thinkers! Put your thinking caps on! (Students pretend to put hats on.) **Why do you**

> **TIP**
>
> Read aloud information about the title of the book of Numbers on page 45 in *What the Bible Is All About for Kids.*

think God wanted the Israelites to spy on the land? Remember, God had already decided to give this land to the Israelites!

Moses selected a man who was well liked and a good leader from each of the 12 tribes. Moses told these men to find out about the land, the people and the food. So off the spies went to find out about the land of Canaan! Spies are thorough at gathering intel (intelligence, or good information). Spies in training, how long do you think this mission was going to take? The spies needed plenty of time to travel into Canaan and find out about the land God had promised to give them!

Spies, Report!

The Israelites waited and waited for the spies to return! While they waited, they probably thought about this wonderful place God was going to give them. They had heard it was a good land, but once the spies returned, they would know JUST how good it was! Spies in training, spies follow orders and have good memories. What do you think the Israelite spies saw in this new land?

Finally the day came when the 12 spies arrived back at the Israelites' camp. Two of the spies were carrying a big pole across their shoulders. On the pole between the men hung the biggest cluster of grapes anyone had ever seen! Other spies had their bags and pockets full of good-tasting pomegranates and figs! This land God had promised was the BEST land ever!

But 10 of the spies told Moses, "This land is amazing. Look at its fruit! BUT the people who live there are strong. Their cities are very large, with big walls. And we even saw giants!" Spies in training, how do you think the spies carried out their mission?

But the spies were divided! Ten of the spies said, "We shouldn't go!" But two of the spies, Joshua and Caleb, told the Israelites something different. Caleb said, "We SHOULD go! We can do it! God will help us." Caleb knew and believed what God had already told them! And so did Joshua.

The Fearful Ten

But what GOD had said and what Caleb and

Big Idea

Even when others choose not to, I will keep trusting God.

Joshua had said didn't change the other spies' minds! Can you believe this, spies in training? Why do you think the 10 spies should have listened to God and to Caleb and Joshua?

The 10 spies had already decided, "We can't beat the people in this land. They're giants! We look like grasshoppers compared to them!"

The words of the 10 spies made the rest of the Israelite people scared! They weren't trusting God. They wept! They griped! They moaned and complained about Moses and even God! The 10 fearful spies had now managed to scare thousands of people! The people were so upset that they decided to get rid of Moses, elect a new leader and go back to Egypt! God's miracles, love and care were forgotten!

> **TIP**
>
> Show Lesson 10 Poster and ask students why they think the spies chose to be so afraid.

The Trusting Two

Moses and Aaron fell flat on their faces, praying to God with all their hearts. Spies in training, why was this a GREAT idea? Meanwhile, Caleb and Joshua tried to get the people to REMEMBER the promise GOD had made. But the people talked about KILLING Moses, Aaron, Caleb and Joshua!

What a problem! What would Moses decide to do now? The Bible says that God had heard everything the people had said. God said they had treated Him with contempt—that means they'd talked about Him as if He didn't matter, as if He had never done anything for them! Now God said that the people would never see the good land—after all, they did not believe God would give it to them! Only the two trusting spies, Caleb and Joshua, and the KIDS—people under 20 years old—would set foot in that amazing land God had promised to give to the Israelites.

Action Plan

Identify words and actions that show I trust in God.

Wrap-Up

The Israelites came SO close to the land that God promised to give them, but most of them never actually got to see it, because they did NOT trust God! But because Caleb and Joshua trusted in God, even when no one else agreed with them, they got to be a part of God's awesome promise!

Read aloud Psalm 56:11. **Sometimes we, like Joshua and Caleb, might be the only one of our friends or family who trust God. But even then we can hold on to what we know is true!** Show chair. **When we sit down, we can trust a chair to hold us. This is just a small reminder of how much we can trust God! God will give us the strength we need to keep believing in Him in difficult situations. This week when you see a chair, remember to trust God. Even when other people don't trust Him, He is always worthy of all our trust!**

Connecting Kids to Jesus

Joshua and Caleb trusted that God would keep His promises. Joshua's life helps us know about Jesus. Joshua's name means "the Lord saves," and if you say "Joshua" in the Greek language, it's "Jesus." Just like God helped the Israelites through Joshua, God saves us all through Jesus!

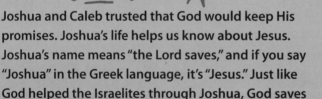

 **(25-30 minutes)**

Whiteboard Time

On whiteboard, draw blank lines for each letter of the first nine words in the Bible verse. **Everyone stand up! Together we are going to write today's Bible verse by guessing letters.** One at a time, students guess letters. If a student is correct, he or she takes a seat. Write letters in the correct blanks on the whiteboard. Once the words are completely filled in, talk about what "trust in God" and "not be afraid" mean. **When we think about situation in our lives, we often don't see things the way God sees them. Even though things can seem scary to us, we can always trust God! God is BIGGER than anything, and He is always trustworthy!**

Distribute Lesson 10 *Kid Talk Cards* and read verse on Side 1 aloud. Students fill in the blanks to find out what Joshua and Caleb said.

▷ **What did Joshua and Caleb see in the land God had promised to them?** (Grapes. Trees. Giants. Walls.)

▷ **What did Joshua and Caleb tell the people they should do?** (Go into the land. Believe God's promise.)

▷ **Why do you think Joshua and Caleb wanted to go into the land even when the others didn't?** (They trusted God. They knew God would help them.)

Students look at Side 2 of *Kid Talk Cards.* Students cross out the picture that shows the wrong action and then circle the picture that shows the response they would choose to do to show their trust in God.

▷ **When might kids want you to do something wrong?** (When they want me to do something I know I'm not allowed to do. When they are making fun of someone who needs help.)

▷ **Why can we trust God? What is He like?** (God is good. He keeps His promises.)

▷ **What are some things you can do to trust God, even when other people aren't trusting Him?** (Remember that God loves me. Pray to Him. Ask for His help to obey His Word. Believe that God's promises are true.)

▷ Show chair. **Like we can trust a chair to hold us when we sit, we can trust God! Even when things seem impossible or scary, God is ALWAYS trustworthy!**

Prayer

Invite volunteers to tell prayer requests as you write them on the whiteboard. Then pray with students about the needs and concerns they mention. Write down the prayer requests of students in your group and pray for them during the week. Next week, let your students know that you have been praying for them.

Art

Ahead of time, use a marker to print in large block letters on separate sheets of white paper each letter of the phrase "We trust in God."

YOU NEED

Markers, white paper, large piece of butcher paper, glue sticks.

Each student chooses one or more of the letters you prepared to decorate with markers. Students put decorated letters in order and then glue decorated letters to large piece of butcher paper to display in classroom.

Connect: **Together, what did we spell? That's right—"We trust in God!" This week, remember to trust God! Even when other people don't trust God, we can keep trusting Him, because we know He will keep His promises, no matter what!**

TIP

Provide stickers, adhesive craft foam shapes or paper scraps for students to arrange in creative designs around letters on butcher paper.

Game

Play a game of Wacky Musical Chairs! Arrange chairs randomly around the room, one fewer chairs than students in your group. As you play music, students walk around the room. When you stop music, students run to sit in chairs. Student who does not find a chair shares

YOU NEED

Chairs, *Worship* CD and player.

a seat with a friend. When all students are sitting, the two students sharing a chair each tell a way to trust God. Remove one chair and play again. This time, two pairs of students will share chairs. Select one of the pairs and have each student tell another way to trust God. Repeat as time permits, removing another chair for each round.

Connect: **Great job! You told some wonderful ways to trust God. Just like you can trust a chair to hold you, you can trust God with ANYTHING in your life! He is always trustworthy! Though other people might worry, we know we can trust God with our lives!**

Get Going

Direct students to look at Side 2 of their *Kid Talk Cards* again. **We never know what might happen, but we DO know that no matter what happens, we can trust God!** Play "I Will Trust in You" (track 4 on *Worship CD*), inviting students to listen or sing along. **This week, remember to trust God with YOUR life!** Distribute Lesson 10 *Family Fridge Fun* papers as students leave.

Moses Strikes Out

Dear Teacher,

It's interesting in today's Bible story that Moses was punished so seriously for striking the rock. Moses had an amazingly close relationship with the Lord. And his frustration with those complaining, accusing Israelites almost seems justified, doesn't it? Why was God so unhappy about Moses' mess-up?

God's words to Moses in Numbers 20:12 help us a little: "You did not trust in me enough to honor me as holy in the sight of the Israelites." Sounds like Moses' anger and disobedience were the result of something else: He didn't TRUST God. Maybe Moses thought that speaking to the rock wouldn't do the trick. Maybe he thought that hitting it, like he'd done 40 years before, would work better. Regardless, he disobeyed because he didn't believe God! Moses teaches a lesson: Obeying God starts with knowing His Word and believing what He says!

Becky English
Editor

Big Idea

I can choose to honor God instead of doing things my own way.

Action Plan

Talk about times I want to have my own way and how I can obey God instead.

Bible Verse

"It is the Lord your God you must follow, and him you must revere. Keep his commands and obey him." Deuteronomy 13:4

Connecting You to Jesus

God provided water for the Israelites, despite the fact that Moses had disobeyed God by striking the rock, instead of speaking to it. God was merciful toward His undeserving, rebellious people. Just like the Israelites did back then, we rebel against God, and we sin by disobeying God's instructions. But God's mercy is made available to us, too—all because God sent Jesus, His Son, to die on the cross to take the punishment for our rebellion.

LESSON MATERIALS

- The basics (see contents)
- Cookies
- Get Thinking—one or two bottles of bubbles, hula hoop
- Story props (see p. 109)
- Materials for Art or Game activity (see pp. 114-115)

Lesson Extras!

1. Help your kids learn the order of books in the Bible by playing Pick and Choose (on CD-ROM). Use the first 22 books of the Old Testament for this lesson.

2. Students learn about today's Bible verse by completing Lesson 11 Bible Verse Puzzle (on CD-ROM).

3. DVD Option: **Just for fun, choose a train and cheer for it!** Show "Lesson 11: Train Race" on *Creative Clips DVD*.

Get Thinking

Welcome students and help them begin to think about today's Big Idea.

Pop!

Place a sheet of construction paper on the floor. Students stand several feet from the paper and take turns blowing bubbles, attempting to make bubbles land and pop on the paper. Move the paper closer or farther away, depending on students' skills. Then hold up a hula hoop and instruct students to take turns attempting to blow bubbles through the hoop.

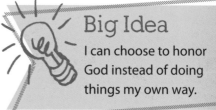

Big Idea

I can choose to honor God instead of doing things my own way.

YOU NEED

Construction paper, one or two bottles of bubbles, hula hoop.

Connect:

▷ **How easy or hard was it to follow my instructions and get your bubbles to go where you wanted them to?**

▷ **Why do you think games have instructions for players to follow?** (So the players understand what to do. So everyone can work together. So someone can win.)

▷ **Today we're going to hear about some instructions that God gave Moses. Moses was supposed to do just what God told him. Let's find out how well Moses did!**

Get God's Word (15-25 minutes)

Moses Strikes Out

Tell the following story summary in your own words, asking discussion questions as indicated.

Story Starter

Point to different corners in the room as you name different choices. Students quickly move to show their choices. **Your ball is stuck in a tree. Should you throw a shoe at it or call the fire department? Your little sister gets gum in her hair. Should you smear peanut butter in her hair or cut the gum out? You forgot to bring your lunch to school. Should you pretend to pass out from hunger or throw a fit? These are silly choices, of course! But sometimes the choices we make can be very important and have serious results. In our story today, God told Moses to do something. We can read what God told Moses to do in Numbers 20:8.** Help students find Numbers 20:8 in their Bibles and find the words "Speak to that rock." **Let's find out what Moses chose to do.**

STORYTELLING IDEA

On whiteboard (or on paper), draw simple pictures from Story Pictures page as instructed throughout story.

We Want Water!

The Israelites had been wandering in the desert for 40 years. That's a long time! Most of the people who had been adults when the Israelites had left Egypt had already died. And the kids at that time were now all grown up!

Every day for all those years, God gave the people food to eat. God had done so many amazing things to take care of His people! But

PEOP GROW KEPTCE 18
DONT ISRSEO 17+6S
GRATFEL NOT PGODS PROVISION NOW
IN YR HEART.

109

TIP

Read aloud the definition of "pomegranate" on page 319 in *What the Bible Is All About for Kids*.

now the people were camped at Kadesh. This was the SAME place the people had camped 40 years before when they had refused to trust God and go into the Promised Land. Draw Story Picture 1.

Do you think these grown-up kids trusted God better than their parents had? Listen as I read Numbers 20:2-5 to find out! In the place where the Israelites were camped, there was no water. So the people got mad at Moses and Aaron and started complaining! "Why did you bring us here to die?" they whined. "This place is terrible! It has no grain or figs or pomegranates or grapevines. And there is no water!" Things hadn't changed much, had they? These people were acting JUST LIKE their parents had!

What do you think Moses and Aaron did about this bunch of thirsty, complaining people? Moses and Aaron knew where to go for help! They did JUST what they had done 40 years before when the people had wanted to KILL Moses, Aaron, Caleb and Joshua! They fell flat on their faces and PRAYED to GOD! Draw Story Picture 2.

God had an answer for them! "Take your staff," God told Moses. "You and Aaron go to that rock you see out there. Draw Story Picture 3. Then, while everyone is watching, speak to the rock. It will pour out water right before everyone's eyes! You will have plenty of water for the people and for all their animals, too."

Moses at the Rock

Moses and Aaron gathered everyone together. Draw Story Picture 4. But Moses was very upset with these people. After all, God had fed and cared for them with miracles ALL their lives, but they were just as selfish and fearful as their parents had been!

Big Idea
I can choose to honor God instead of doing things my own way.

Even though Moses knew what God wanted him to do, Moses did NOT turn to the rock and speak to it. Instead, he yelled at the people, "Listen, you rebels! Do WE have to bring water out of this ROCK for you?" Then he hit the rock as hard as he could twice! Water POURED out of the rock. Draw Story Picture 5.

TIP

Show Lesson 11 Poster and ask students how they think the people felt when Moses got angry and struck the rock.

Even though the people had bad attitudes and Moses lost his temper and disobeyed, God still made water come out of that rock. God showed kindness, even though the Israelites did not deserve it!

So now everyone had enough to drink, and the people were happy! But God was NOT happy with Moses. **Why do you think God was unhappy with Moses?** Moses had been told to SPEAK to the rock, not whack it as hard as he could! He had disobeyed God's instructions and acted in anger and pride. Remember what Moses had said? "Do WE have to bring water out of this rock?" Moses forgot that GOD was the One who would make water come out. So God told Moses and Aaron that neither of them would lead the Israelites into the Promised Land. That was sad. Draw Story Picture 6.

After 40 years, the Israelites still didn't REALLY trust God, even after eating manna every day! That was sad, too. But God didn't stop loving His people. He never gave up on them.

Wrap-Up

Moses loved God and usually obeyed Him, but when the Israelites complained against him AGAIN, Moses got frustrated. He was so tired of the Israelites always complaining that he got mad and did things his own way, but that did not honor God. We're like that sometimes! When people make us upset or we don't like what we're asked to do, we sometimes get mad and do things our own way. Then it can be hard to act in ways that honor God.

Show cookies. **Have you ever wanted something that you couldn't have? Maybe you wanted a cookie, but your mom said no! Honoring God means choosing to obey His commands, even if we feel frustrated about things we don't like.** Read Deuteronomy 13:4 aloud. **All the great things God has done for us help us want to love and honor and obey Him with all our hearts.**

Action Plan

Talk about times I want to have my own way and how I can obey God instead.

Connecting Kids to Jesus

God provided water for the Israelites, even though Moses had disobeyed God by striking the rock instead of speaking to it. God showed mercy to His rebellious people. Today, when we disobey God's instructions, we sin just like the Israelites did. But God shows mercy to us, too! God sent Jesus, His Son, to die on the cross to take the punishment for our sins.

Get Talking  **(25-30 minutes)**

Whiteboard Time

On whiteboard, draw a large footprint. **Our verse today tells us ways to FOLLOW God!** Read Deuteronomy 13:4 aloud and ask students to listen for action words and phrases. Whenever they hear an action ("follow," "revere," "keep commands" and "obey"), students clap hands. As volunteers tell the action they heard, print the words on or around footprint. **God is really worth obeying! All the great things God has done make me want to love and honor Him. You can also choose to love and honor Him, just like our verse says to do!**

Distribute Lesson 11 *Kid Talk Cards* and read Bible verse aloud. Students look at picture of Moses on Side 1 and then draw something Moses could have done to obey God instead.

▷ **How did the Israelites show that they wanted their own way?** (They complained. They blamed Moses for their problems. They did not trust God to take care of them.)

▷ **Why do you think Moses chose to disobey God by hitting the rock?** (He was angry.)

▷ **What happened after Moses and Aaron disobeyed?** (God said they could not go into the Promised Land.)

Students look at Side 2 of *Kid Talk Cards*. Students circle the picture that shows a kid obeying God. Then students write a prayer asking God to help them obey.

▷ Point to photo of cookies. **Sometimes it's OK to have a cookie, isn't it? But if your mom says you can't have one, then it would be wrong to take one. It's the same way with God. He asks us to do certain things because He loves us, and He wants us to respect Him and obey His commands.**

▷ **Who are some people you know who show honor and respect to God?**

▷ **What are some times you might want your own way, and how could you obey God instead?** (Do homework when you'd rather play, be kind if a friend hurts your feelings, do your chores without complaining, etc.)

Prayer

Invite volunteers to tell prayer requests as you write them on the whiteboard. Then pray with students about the needs and concerns they mention. Invite students to silently talk to God about times they have disobeyed Him. End prayer time by thanking God for loving us and forgiving us when we disobey.

Art

Give each student a rock. Students use light-colored crayons to color their rocks, working the color into any grooves and cracks. Students then use a dark-colored crayon to write words or phrases from the Bible verse. Students decorate the rest of the rock as they desire.

YOU NEED

Bibles, one smooth fist-sized rock for each student, crayons.

Connect: **Every day there are times I can choose to honor God and follow Him. You can make that choice, too. During the week, look at your rock as a reminder to honor God!**

TIP

If possible, warm rocks in an oven before giving them to students (be careful not to get rocks too hot!). Students color warmed rocks with crayons to create a smoother covering and a brighter color with the crayons.

Game

Divide class into two teams. Both teams line up on one side of the room. Place the bowl of beans at the opposite side of the room. Place an empty bowl in front of each team, and give the first player on each team a spoon. When you say go, first player on each team walks to the bowl of beans and scoops a spoonful of beans to bring back to his or her team's bowl. Each team member takes a turn scooping beans and returning the beans to his or her team's bowl. Students take multiple turns, continuing game until large bean bowl is empty or until you call time. The team with the most beans in its bowl wins.

> **YOU NEED**
>
> Large bowl of dry beans, two small bowls, two plastic spoons.

Connect: **We had to follow the rules to make this game work, didn't we? Obeying the rules makes a game fun for everybody! It's even more important for us to obey God's commands. I'll be praying for you this week that God will help you choose to honor Him by obeying Him.**

Get Going

Direct students to look at Side 2 of their *Kid Talk Cards* again. **When God tells us to obey Him, it's always for our own good. Let's sing about how He wants us to live!** Play "God's Top 10" (track 3 on *Worship CD*), inviting students to listen or sing along. **This week, let's remember to honor God by choosing to do the things He wants us to do!** Distribute Lesson 11 *Family Fridge Fun* papers as students leave.

Surprised by Snakes

Dear Teacher,

As a kid, my big brother wanted to be a herpetologist—a snake expert. So I've never been afraid of snakes; it's just important to "avoid the sharp end"!

Sometimes, my own sinful rebellion against God reminds me of my attitude toward snakes. I think I can let my sin of complaining mistrust slither around as long as I avoid getting bitten. But like the snakes God sent to the Israelites, these attitudes always bite. In my case, though, the poison doesn't kill, but it does infect my soul.

Fortunately for both the Israelites and myself, God responds to a confession of sin with forgiveness and salvation. Just as the poisoned, dying Israelites could look at the bronze snake and be healed, I can look to Jesus and be forgiven for my sins—healed of the poisonous infection caused by my distrustful complaining!

Mary Davis
Senior Editor

Big Idea

When I've sinned, I can accept God's forgiveness and turn away from doing wrong.

Action Plan

Become part of God's family as the Holy Spirit leads, and identify situations in which God's forgiveness is needed.

Bible Verse

"Whoever believes in the Son has eternal life, but whoever rejects the Son will not see life, for God's wrath remains on him." John 3:36

Connecting You to Jesus

The Israelites experienced God's forgiveness by following His instructions to look up at a bronze snake Moses had built on a pole. God's forgiveness meant that they would not die from the bites of the snakes God had sent as punishment for their complaints. Like the Israelites, we all experience the consequences of sin, which ultimately mean death. The only way we can live is by looking to the perfect One who was lifted up on the cross to take the penalty of death upon Himself. If we look on Jesus, our Savior, we will live forever!

LESSON MATERIALS

- The basics (see contents)
- Toy snake
- Get Thinking—crayons or markers
- Story Starter—Complaints page (from CD-ROM)
- Materials for Art or Game activity (see pp. 124-125)

Lesson Extras!

1. Help your kids learn the order of books in the Bible by playing Book Pass (on CD-ROM). Use the first 27 books of the Old Testament for this lesson.

2. Students talk about today's Bible story as they complete Lesson 12 Bible Story Coloring Page (on CD-ROM).

3. DVD Option: **What if someone forgave you, but you didn't accept that forgiveness? How crazy would that look?** Show "Lesson 12: Forgive Me" on *Creative Clips DVD*. **The great news is that God really has forgiven us, and we can accept His forgiveness!**

Get Thinking

Welcome students and help them begin to think about today's Big Idea.

Drawing on Memory

Line up 15 or more crayons or markers in a row. Encourage students to look closely at the row for about 30 seconds. Then students close their eyes while you quickly remove one of the crayons or markers. Students open their eyes and attempt to tell which color was removed. Repeat, inviting a student to remove one the next time.

Big Idea

When I've sinned, I can accept God's forgiveness and turn away from doing wrong.

YOU NEED

Crayons or markers.

Connect:

▷ **What did you do to remember which colors of crayons were here?**

▷ **What are some other things you do to remember things?** (Write down what I want to remember, talk about it, repeat it over and over, draw a picture about it, etc.)

▷ **Today we'll be talking about one of the most important things to remember in the whole world!**

Get God's Word (15-25 minutes)

Surprised by Snakes

Tell the following story summary in your own words, asking discussion questions as indicated.

Story Starter

Ahead of time, cut apart Complaints page and place strips in a bag.

I need a volunteer! Volunteer takes a strip of paper from bag and reads it aloud. **If you have said this, jump up in the air! Would you call this a big complaint or a little complaint?** Students respond.

> **YOU NEED**
>
> Bible for yourself and each student, Complaints page (from CD-ROM), Lesson 12 Poster, scissors, bag, toy snake.

Then invite another volunteer to take another strip and read it aloud. Continue until all the strips have been read. **These complaints are about situations that lots of kids might want to complain about. Some people in our story today felt that they had a good reason to complain, too! Look at Numbers 21:5 to find out what they started to complain about.** Help students find Numbers 21:5 in their Bibles and point to the words "water" and "food." **Let's find out what happened!**

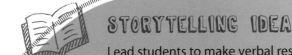

STORYTELLING IDEA

Lead students to make verbal responses to actions as directed during the story.

Lessons Learned?

The Israelites were traveling, slowly moving closer and closer to the land God had promised to give them. They had been forced to travel around the territory of the Edomites, who would not let them pass through their country. Lead students to say "Uh-oh!"

TIP

Show Lesson 12 Poster and ask students to describe what is happening in the picture.

It was hot. It was dry. Traveling wasn't fun after 40 years of it. God's people were cranky and impatient. **Can you guess what these cranky and impatient people did?** Yep, they started to complain! Lead students to say "Grumble, grumble, grumble!"

Even though the Israelites were tired and impatient, they STILL had enough energy to COMPLAIN. They accused Moses of bringing them out to DIE in the desert. **And what did they say about the perfect, miraculous food God had been giving them every day for 40 years?** "We HATE this MISERABLE FOOD!" Lead students to repeat "Grumble, grumble, grumble!"

Even though the people had seen God take care of their needs over and over and OVER—even though they had MANY memories of MIRACLES when God had given them food and water—they weren't grateful! All of their memories were chased away by their worries about what they wanted RIGHT NOW. Lead students to repeat "Grumble, grumble, grumble!"

Surprised by Snakes!

The Israelites were so caught up in their complaining that they couldn't think of anything else. They said that God's GOOD gifts were BAD. They told Moses that he was a rotten leader. They were all wrapped up in their own misery like THOUSANDS of wailing babies! Lead students to say "Wah, wah, wah!"

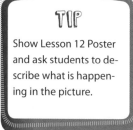

But suddenly, the people were SURPRISED! SNAKES were everywhere! THAT got their ATTENTION! And the snakes weren't garden snakes. They were POISONOUS snakes! Lead students to say "Uh-oh!"

When those snakes showed up, their poisonous bites reminded the people that God had HEARD their mean, poisonous words against Him. The snakebites were DEADLY, and people started to DIE!

Big Idea

When I've sinned, I can accept God's forgiveness and turn away from doing wrong.

What do you think the people did and said? The Israelites didn't have any trouble connecting their horrible words and attitudes with the fact that there were snakes everywhere! They knew they had sinned! They asked Moses to pray, and he did. Lead students to say "Help us, God!" But God told Moses to do something very unusual.

TIP

Read aloud information about the bronze serpent at the top of page 46 in *What the Bible Is All About for Kids*. Explain that it is a picture of Jesus Christ.

God's Solution

Listen as I read Numbers 21:8 to hear God's unusual instructions. God could have just healed everyone. But God's plan was a special way to show His love!

So Moses obeyed God. He made a snake out of metal and put it up on a pole. Then the people had to make a choice. Those people who didn't believe God's instructions could choose to not look at the snake and they would die. But anyone who was willing to look at the bronze snake would not die. That person would be healed of his or her snakebite! Lead students to say "Hurray!"

Wrap-Up

Moses and the people must have been so glad that God provided a way for them to be healed of their snakebites! When they were healed, they knew that God still loved them and that their sins were forgiven. Just like the Israelites, we sin, too. We disobey God. The good news is that although God doesn't take away the consequences of our wrong actions, He does promise to forgive us when we believe in Jesus.

Action Plan

Become part of God's family as the Holy Spirit leads, and identify situations in which God's forgiveness is needed.

When Jesus lived on Earth, He talked about this time when the Israelites showed their faith by looking at the bronze snake (see John 3:14-15). Show toy snake. **Jesus said that when we believe in Jesus as God's Son and believe that He died to take the punishment for our sins, then God gladly forgives our sins and we become members of God's family.** Read John 3:36 aloud. **We each have a choice to reject Jesus or to accept Him.** Talk with interested students about becoming members of God's family (see "Connecting Kids to Jesus" on pp. 3-5).

Connecting Kids to Jesus

The Israelites had sinned against God, and without God's forgiveness, they would have died from the bites of the poisonous snakes. But God forgave the Israelites when they looked up at the bronze snake Moses had built on a pole. In the same way, we sin and need God to forgive us, too. The only way we can be forgiven is to look to Jesus, the One who died on the cross to take the punishment for our sin. If we admit our sin and believe in Jesus as our Savior, we will live forever with Him.

Get Talking (25-30 minutes)

Whiteboard Time

On whiteboard, draw and label picture as shown, leaving off the cross and "Believe in Jesus." **What did God's Son, Jesus, do so that we can have eternal life with God?** Read John 3:36 aloud. Draw a cross to connect "us" and "God." **What do we need to do to accept this gift?** Add the words "Believe in Jesus." **You can choose to believe in Jesus and accept God's forgiveness. It's the best choice to make!**

Distribute Lesson 12 *Kid Talk Cards*. Read the Bible verse aloud. **God wanted the Israelites to admit their sin and accept His forgiveness.** On Side 1, students use the code to complete the sentence about what the Israelites chose to do.

▷ **What choices did the Israelites make during this story? What were the results of their choices?** (They were bitten by snakes. They were made well when they looked at the bronze snake.)

▷ **How did the Israelites show belief in God?**

▷ **What happened to Jesus when He lived on Earth that reminds us of the bronze snake being placed on a pole?** (Jesus died on the cross to take the punishment for our sins.)

Students turn to Side 2 of *Kid Talk Cards*. Students follow the path to find things to pray about. Lead students in praying about each item on the path.

▷ **When is a time a kid would need God's forgiveness at school? At home?**

▷ **What's another way to say "has eternal life"?** (Lives forever as part of God's family. Has life with God.) **"Will not see life"?** (Will not be a part of God's family.)

▷ Point to photo of snake and read aloud the words on the picture. **What would you like to know about becoming a member of God's family?**

Prayer

Invite volunteers to tell prayer requests as you write them on the whiteboard. Then pray with students about the needs and concerns they mention. Remember that some children will easily pray aloud, while others simply listen. This doesn't mean they are not praying! Accept each child's level of participation.

Art

On a large sheet of paper, print "God loves and forgives me!"

Give each student a Sun Shape Pattern. Students cut out shape and attach collage materials with glue stick, covering the shape. When collage is completed, students use permanent markers to copy words from large sheet of paper onto the sun shape to make a reminder.

Connect: **I'm so glad that God made a way to forgive us and to make us part of His family! Remembering what God has done for me makes me want to obey Him.**

YOU NEED

One Sun Shape Pattern (from CD-ROM) printed on card stock for each student, large sheet of paper, marker, scissors, a variety of collage materials (tissue paper, scrapbooking paper scraps, etc.), glue sticks, permanent markers.

TIP

For larger collages, copy Sun Shape Pattern onto poster-board sheets and cut out one for each student.

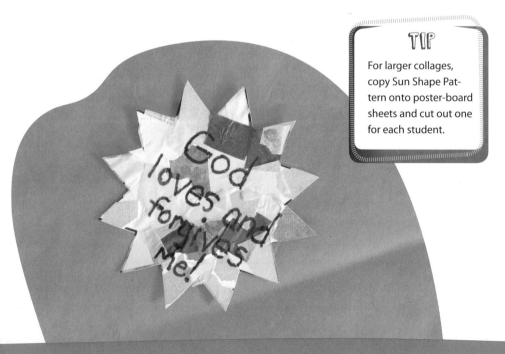

Game

Ahead of time, on three separate sheets of construction paper, print "Bible Verse." On other sheets of construction paper, print "Tell a time to ask for forgiveness," "Tell a reason to thank God," "Spin around," "Jump," "Clap hands" and "Hop on one foot." Arrange papers in a grid pattern. Make a masking-tape line several feet from the grid.

YOU NEED

Bibles, nine sheets of construction paper, marker, masking tape, three or more beanbags.

Divide group into two teams. Teams stand behind masking-tape line and take turns tossing beanbag onto the grid. Depending on where beanbag lands, team says the Bible verse, tells a time to ask for forgiveness, tells a reason to thank God or leads the whole group in doing the action described. Team attempts to get three beanbags in a row before the next team takes a turn. Continue playing several rounds.

Connect: **God loves us so much! And His forgiveness is amazing! Even though we have done wrong things, God forgives us because of what Jesus did when He died on the cross and came back to life again!**

Get Going

Direct students to look at Side 2 of their *Kid Talk Cards* again. **Read the prayer you wrote as you listen to this song.** Play "I Will Trust in You" (track 4 on *Worship CD*), inviting students to listen or sing along. **God loves you more than you can imagine! He is glad to invite you to be part of His family forever.** Distribute Lesson 12 *Family Fridge Fun* papers as students leave.

One Smart Donkey

Dear Teacher,

As I read the Scripture passage for this lesson, I was struck by how important our hearts are to God! And unlike humans who see "but a poor reflection as in a mirror," God sees the human heart in its entirety (1 Corinthians 13:12).

It is easy for us to make conclusions based on behaviors that we see. But how does the Lord judge? When God spoke to Samuel, He was clear: "The Lord does not look at the things man looks at. Man looks at the outward appearance, but the Lord looks at the heart" (1 Samuel 16:7). God cares about much more than our external actions; He also cares about our heart attitudes!

What is the condition of your heart? This week, FULLY surrender your heart to the Lord. Where needed, let God revive your heart. The condition of our hearts matters to our God—let's live like it!

Kristina Fucci
Assistant Editor

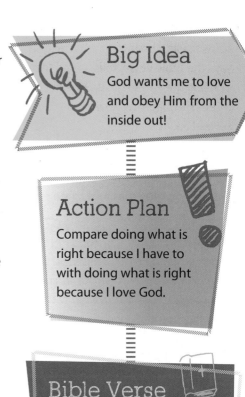

Big Idea

God wants me to love and obey Him from the inside out!

Action Plan

Compare doing what is right because I have to with doing what is right because I love God.

Bible Verse

"Love the Lord your God, listen to his voice, and hold fast to him. For the Lord is your life." Deuteronomy 30:20

Connecting You to Jesus

Balaam was hired to curse God's people, but God would not let Balaam do that. Instead, Balaam blessed Israel when God's Spirit spoke through him! Balaam's blessing also contains a distinct prophecy about Jesus, the Messiah: "A star will come out of Jacob; a scepter will rise out of Israel" (Numbers 24:17). God used Balaam not only to bless Israel but also to announce His plan of salvation to the whole world. God's plan to bless His people cannot be stopped by any enemy!

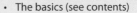

LESSON MATERIALS

- The basics (see contents)
- Box of chocolates
- Get Thinking—play dough
- Story Starter—puppet
- Story props (see p. 129)
- Materials for Art or Game activity (see pp. 134-135)

Lesson Extras!

1. Help your kids learn the order of books in the Bible by playing Book Pass (on CD-ROM). Use the first 27 books of the Old Testament for this lesson.

2. Students talk about today's Bible verse as they complete Lesson 13 Bible Verse Coloring Page (on CD-ROM).

3. DVD Option: **Let's watch this video and see how fast we can memorize Deuteronomy 30:20.** Show "Lesson 13: Mission Memorization" on *Creative Clips DVD*. **This verse is a wonderful reminder of how we can love and obey God with our entire lives.**

Get Thinking

(10-15 minutes)

Welcome students and help them begin to think about today's Big Idea.

Shape Your Thoughts

As students arrive, give each one a fist-sized ball of play dough and invite them to shape something that they like to think about. **All of us have things we like to think about! See if you can shape something that lets other people know things that you are thinking of.**

Big Idea

God wants me to love and obey Him from the inside out!

YOU NEED

Play dough.

Connect:

▷ **What are some of the things you made? How many different kinds of things were people in our class thinking about?**

▷ **What are some ways that people can know what you are thinking?** (You can tell them. By the way you act.)

▷ **Today we're going to hear about someone who tried to HIDE what he was thinking. He acted like he was doing good, but what he was thinking about was NOT good. Let's find out what he was thinking and doing!**

Get God's Word (15-25 minutes)

One Smart Donkey

Tell the following story summary in your own words, asking questions as indicated.

Story Starter

Pretend to be a ventriloquist (talk without moving your lips) and use a puppet (or a sock on your hand) to welcome students. It's perfectly OK if you are not convincing as a ventriloquist and end up laughing with students! **Could you tell who was talking? Did I fool you at all?** Students respond. **In our story today, something that wasn't supposed to talk started talking—and it was for real! It is written about in Numbers 22. Numbers is the fourth book in the Bible.** Help students find Numbers 22 in their Bibles. **Let's find out what happened.**

> ## YOU NEED
>
> Bible for yourself and each student, Lesson 13 Poster, Donkey Dialogue (from CD-ROM), person puppet, donkey puppet, box of chocolates.

STORYTELLING IDEA

Print Donkey Dialogue (from CD-ROM). Invite an adult volunteer uses puppets and Donkey Dialogue to act out story action as directed throughout the story.

Say What God Says

The Israelites had traveled and traveled. Now they were camped on the plains of Moab—next to the Promised Land! But the people of Moab and their friends the Midianites were NOT happy about this mass of people who had filled part of their land. They were TERRIFIED that the Israelites were going to take over their land! How could they get RID of such a HUGE group of people?

King Balak came up with a bright idea. He sent messengers to ask a man named Balaam to come and put a CURSE on the Israelites! **Why do you think he did such a terrible thing?** Now Balaam did NOT follow the one true God. No, Balaam was more like what we could call a fortune-teller, and people paid him to curse or bless others!

TIP

Read aloud the definition of the word "curse" on page 300 and the word "bless" on page 296 in *What the Bible Is All About for Kids*.

The messengers brought money to pay Balaam and told him their mission. Balaam invited the men to spend the night and told them he'd give them God's answer in the morning. That night, God said to Balaam, "Do not go with them. You must not curse the Israelites!" So in the morning, Balaam told the men what God had said and sent them back to the king.

But soon, MORE messengers came from King Balak! They had the SAME request. They, too, spent the night and waited for God's answer. This time, God told Balaam to go with the men but to say and do only what GOD SAID to say and do. So Balaam got on his donkey and went. But God knew that Balaam did NOT want to do what God had said to do. Balaam really wanted to do what King Balak had asked him to do!

Who Said That?

Volunteer holds Balaam and Donkey puppets. As Balaam rode along, his donkey suddenly saw something that Balaam could NOT see! The angel of the Lord stood in the road with a sword in his hand! **Why do you think Balaam couldn't see the angel?** The scared donkey turned off the road into a field. She was NOT going to run into an angel with a sword! Donkey puppet turns to the side. But Balaam, angrily smacked the poor donkey until she got back on the road. Balaam puppet hits donkey puppet, and then they continue forward.

The angel moved ahead and stood in front of them again, this time in a narrow place with walls on both sides of the road. The donkey had nowhere to turn, so she pressed up against a wall and crushed Balaam's foot! Donkey puppet pins Balaam puppet against wall. Balaam beat her again in his anger and pain. He didn't even stop to wonder why she was acting strangely! Balaam puppet hits donkey puppet, and then they continue forward.

Then the angel moved ahead and stood where there was no wiggle room at ALL! When the donkey looked up and saw the angel, she just LAY

Big Idea
God wants me to love and obey Him from the inside out!

DOWN in the road. Donkey puppet lies down. Balaam was FURIOUS! He started hitting her again—this time with a stick! Balaam puppet hits donkey puppet energetically. So God did something to get Balaam's attention: He made the donkey TALK!

Donkey puppet speaks to Balaam puppet. "What have I done to make you beat me three times? Do I usually act like this?"

Then God opened Balaam's eyes to see the angel. Balaam bowed low and lay facedown! Balaam puppet bows down.

> **TIP**
>
> Show Lesson 13 Poster and ask students what they think the DONKEY is thinking.

Then the angel said to him, "What you are thinking and planning is putting you in danger!" He reminded Balaam of God's warning: "Go. But speak ONLY what I tell you." God knew Balaam's heart!

What Can I Say?

When Balaam finally met with King Balak, they went to stand on a mountainside and look down at the Israelites camped below. **What do you think Balaam was going to do?** The king kept telling Balaam to curse the Israelites. **But listen as I read Numbers 24:8-9 to hear out what Balaam said about Israel.** God only let Balaam say blessings and tell the good things that God wanted for the Israelites.

Finally Balaam left. But even though he had SAID what God wanted him to say, Balaam still did not love God! In fact, he spent the rest of his life trying to cause trouble for the Israelites.

Wrap-Up

We've all acted like Balaam at times. We've obeyed someone because we had to, but inside we were feeling unhappy or stubborn. How much better it is when we obey someone and do what is right because we WANT to, not just because we HAVE to!

Show box of chocolates. **The chocolates in this box all look good on the outside, but sometimes the insides aren't what we want!** Read Deuteronomy 30:19-20. **Sometimes we are a little bit like chocolates! Our outsides—the things we do—look good, but our insides—our thoughts—are not**

Action Plan

Compare doing what is right because I have to with doing what is right because I love God.

good. God cares about us and wants both our insides and our outsides to be good. And we start to do that by loving God. God will help us listen to Him and think right thoughts and do right things. That's how we love and obey Him from the inside out!

Connecting Kids to Jesus

Balaam was paid to curse God's people, but God would not let Balaam do that. Instead, God told Balaam what to say, and Balaam said good things about Israel! Besides that, Balaam even talked about Jesus, the coming Savior. God used Balaam to bless Israel and also to tell the whole world about His plan of salvation for ALL people—including you and me! No enemy can stop God's plans to do good to His people!

Get Talking (25-30 minutes)

Whiteboard Time

Our verse today tells us how to obey God from the inside out! On whiteboard, volunteer draws a hand. Read Deuteronomy 30:20 aloud, pausing after each punctuation mark, so students hear four distinct phrases. Ask students which phrase matches the hand ("hold fast to him"). **Yes, that's right! Good job!** Invite volunteers, one at a time, to draw a heart, a stick figure person and an ear, stopping after each drawing to reread verse and let students discover each matching phrase (heart—"love the Lord your God"; stick figure—"He is your life"; ear—"listen to his voice"). **When we love God, listen to Him and hold fast to Him, we will WANT to live our whole lives for Him!**

Distribute Lesson 13 *Kid Talk Cards*. On Side 1, students draw the picture that shows why Balaam wanted to do what the king wanted. Then students use the code to find out what Balaam had to do instead.

▷ **What did Balaam do?** (He said the things God told him to say.) **What did he really WANT to do?** (He wanted to do what King Balak asked and curse God's people.)

▷ **What might have been different if Balaam had loved God?**

Students look at Side 2 of *Kid Talk Cards*. Students compare the attitudes shown by the kids in the pictures. Students write a prayer asking God to help them do what is right because of their love for Him.

▷ Point to photo of box of chocolates. **We can't always tell by looking at the outside of a chocolate what it's like on the inside—and what's on the inside makes a big difference! God cares about what we are like on the inside AND on the outside! He wants us to love Him with our thoughts AND actions.**

▷ **What are ways we can love God?** (Pray to God when we wake up, help another kid, etc.) **How can we listen to God's voice?** (Read the Bible, go to church, etc.) **How can we hold fast to God?** (Don't give up doing what is right, etc.)

▷ **What do you think "the Lord is your life" means?** (We want to live for Him.)

Prayer

Talk about your own prayer life—when you pray, how, if you use a journal, etc. This will help kids see that prayer is a daily part of following Jesus. Invite volunteers to tell prayer requests as you write them on the whiteboard. Then pray with students about the needs and concerns they mention.

Art

Ahead of time, write the words "Love God— inside and out!" on large sheet of paper, so students can later copy them.

Give each student one Donkey Pattern page and one sheet of colored card stock. Students cut out pieces from pattern. Students glue pieces on sheet of card stock to create a donkey. Students trim off any paper that hangs over edges and then glue on google eyes. Students cut 1-inch (2.5-cm) pieces of yarn and glue them along the donkey's neck and head to make a mane. Somewhere on their paper, students copy the words "Love God—inside and out!"

> ### YOU NEED
>
> One Donkey Pattern page (from CD-ROM) printed on brown card stock for each student, large sheet of paper, markers, one sheet of colored card stock for each student, scissors, glue, google eyes, yarn.

Connect: **It's kind of funny that in our story today, the only one who did what was right was a donkey! God wants us to do what's right, too—not because we have to, but because we love Him.**

> ### TIP
>
> If you do not have google eyes, students can draw eyes with markers.

Game

Today we're going to play a game a little like Freeze Tag! But instead of running, you are going to stay in one place. Tell students that you will play music, and when the music starts, they can dance or move in place. When the music stops, they should freeze. Student who freezes last tells a way to do what is right (be honest, let a friend choose first, keep a promise to parents, etc.). Repeat as time and interest allow.

YOU NEED

Music CD and player.

Connect: **When we obey only because we HAVE to, we aren't really very happy. God knows that when we love Him and listen to Him, we will WANT to obey. And loving God is the best way to live!**

Get Going

Direct students to look at Side 2 of their *Kid Talk Cards* again. **There is only one true God! He wants us to love Him with our whole hearts!** Play "One True God" (track 6 on *Worship CD*), inviting students to listen or sing along. **Let's remember this week to listen to God's voice and hold fast to Him. Then we will love and obey Him from the inside out!** Distribute Lesson 13 *Family Fridge Fun* papers as students leave.